EVIL
FAMILIES

EVIL FAMILIES

A History of Bad Blood

Martin Knight

This edition published in 2021 by Arcturus Publishing Limited
26/27 Bickels Yard, 151–153 Bermondsey Street,
London SE1 3HA

AD006867UK

Printed in the UK

Contents

Introduction

The family is a subversive organization.
Ferdinand Mount, The Subversive Family

Most of us find it easier to relate to the warring broods of TV soap operas than to the idealized picture of family life depicted in sentimental movies, period novels and vintage TV series.

It's a depressing fact that the 'average' family is likely to be a battleground of incompatible personalities divided by conflicting interests and beset by the constant stress of living together.

In fact, today there is no such thing as the 'average' family. Single parents, single-sex partnerships and families unrelated by

Local aristocracy: notorious London mobsters the Kray twins take a stroll on their home patch. Ronnie and Reggie's gang was known as 'The Firm' and they did a little bit of everything: murder, protection rackets, armed robbery and GBH. In their spare time, they mixed with politicians and celebrities of the day.

blood or marriage are no longer the exception but commonplace.

Sadly, whatever their background and culture, a number of children feel compelled to conform to their parents' expectations and believe they have to measure themselves by society's standards of success, but all too frequently they fall short of those ideals. Some people cope better than others under pressure. Many, however, resort to antidepressants, alcohol or drugs, which only exacerbates the problem. A rare few are given the opportunity to talk through their troubles in counselling, but it takes a degree of self-awareness to admit to being unable to cope with the stress of family life and tragically many individuals at some point suffer some form of breakdown. This can involve violence against themselves or towards those they live with. Those who internalize their problems may ultimately turn on their own families, with dire and often fatal consequences. They might murder their partners and even their own children after suffering a 'psychic break' which subsequently leaves them in denial of their crimes. One part of their mind simply cannot accept that they have committed those monstrous acts.

Those who externalize their rage and resentment can become 'neighbours from hell', whose antisocial behaviour is the bane of the community. In time, the more dysfunctional and psychologically scarred may graduate to serious crime. They have no regard for the effect their actions will have on their victims, for they lack both a conscience and any conception of the consequences.

UK crime families

The Messina brothers – five Maltese brothers who reigned over an empire of vice and extortion in London's Soho during the 1950s – were raised to believe that extortion and exploiting the vulnerability of others was an acceptable means of doing business. They shared the delusion that they were above the law and boasted that they were 'more powerful than the British Government'.

They were succeeded by the Kray Twins, Ronnie and Reggie, for whom violence was a way of life, not merely a means of dissuading their rivals from muscling in on their criminal empire. When Ronnie died in March 1995, his body was driven through the East End of London, where local inhabitants lined the pavements to pay silent homage to the man they believed had kept the streets safe for women and children.

The twins were perceived as being victims of an abusive and impoverished upbringing – 'lovable rogues' who only preyed on their own kind – but Ronnie, who was diagnosed as a paranoid schizophrenic and certified insane, and his brother Reggie presided over a criminal empire enforced with violence and intimidation.

North of the border, the Daniel and Lyons families carried on a lethal and brutal turf war in Glasgow's Milton district during the 1990s, allegedly protected by corrupt local politicians and the police, while their counterparts in the south continued to swagger and strut like characters from *Lock, Stock and Two Smoking Barrels*, defying the law to cut them down to size.

The culture of ultra-violence still dominates inner-city crime in Britain, but in the new millennium the stakes are higher and the profits from illegal drugs are far in excess of what the Krays could ever have dreamed of. Crime provides these families with an easy living, an alternative to conventional employment, potential wealth beyond their dreams and a false sense of superiority. They may even delude themselves into believing that they have the 'respect' of those who submit out of fear.

Carmelo Messina celebrates his acquittal by a Belgian court in 1956. He and his four brothers were part of a Malta-based crime organization that ran a prostitution racket in central London during the inter-war and post-war years. Protected by bent policemen and other officials, they imported sex workers from Belgium, France and Spain. By the late 1940s, they were operating at least 30 brothels in the capital. One of the brothers, Attilio, said: 'We Messinas are more powerful than the British government. We do as we like in England.'

Living like drug lords

On the other side of the world the South American drug lords portray themselves as devoted family men and flaunt their prodigious wealth and extravagant lifestyles as proof that they have what it takes to rise above the poverty into which they have been born.

Mexican drug baron Amado Carrillo Fuentes was initiated into the lucrative drug business by his uncle Ernesto, who then became his mentor. Amado later brought in his brothers and eventually his son, Vicente José Carrillo Leyva.

Arturo Beltrán Leyva, the self-proclaimed Mexican cocaine king, engaged in a bitter and bloody feud with his rival Joaquín Guzmán, despite the fact that they were related. Arturo argued that his five younger brothers depended on the income from his narcotics business, and so the fact that he was related to his competitor should not be permitted to interfere with business.

Further north, Mickey Mo believed that violence was the only means of ensuring loyalty from his Oakland, California criminal family firm, until his arrest. Then the 'born again' drug kingpin ditched the baseball bat for the Bible and now preaches against the evils of heroin.

All drug dealers are in it for the short term, seemingly oblivious to the sobering fact that many will end up dead or in jail before they see middle age.

They may live in vulgar, ostentatious luxury, but they also live in fear, not only of death or prison but also of betrayal. None appear to have twigged to the truth that there is only so much money you can spend in a lifetime and that eventually they will have to bury the excess cash, as Pablo Escobar was forced to do when he had far exceeded his wildest dreams of making money.

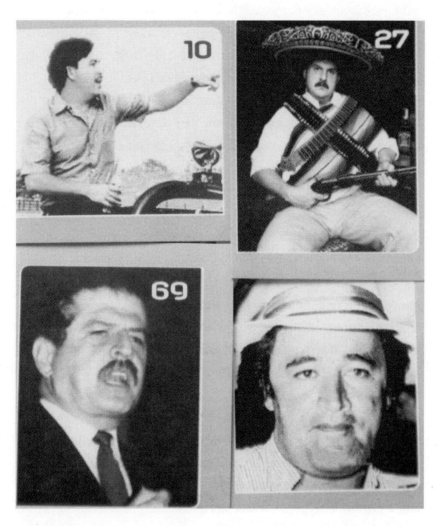

In 2012, cashing in on the success of a Colombian soap opera called Pablo the Evil Boss, *somebody produced this curious sticker album to commemorate Pablo Escobar's life and crimes.*

Evil is as evil does

Evil families are not a modern phenomenon. Madness and murder characterized the lives of the 12 hereditary Caesars in ancient Rome; the Ming dynasty of ancient China cultivated cruelty as an art form; while the Tudor kings ruled England with an iron fist, slaughtering their own to ensure their sovereignty endured during some of the bloodiest episodes in English history. The Borgias, too, consolidated their stranglehold on Renaissance Italy, using bribery and blackmail and not stinting on the assassinations.

The New World inherited many of the sins of the old, with numerous clans of murderous scavengers and thieves terrorizing the lawless frontier in the Wild West, having escaped from Europe where they or their ancestors had fallen foul of the authorities.

Long before the West went wild, the Harpe brothers of Kentucky were slaughtering unsuspecting settlers, ripping open their torsos while they were still breathing and filling their chests with rocks before sinking them in the river. You didn't want to come across them on a dark night when there wasn't a lawman for miles to hear your screams and ride to the rescue.

Their neighbours, the 'Bloody Benders' of Kansas, offered their guests room and board for one night only at their travellers' inn in the 1870s, while the Kelly family – mother, father, son and daughter – were just one short of ratcheting up a round dozen killings at their family inn when their collar was felt by the long arm of the law.

But the tallies of both looked meagre compared to the Stafflebacks, also from Kansas, who disposed of around 50 strangers, all of them customers of a local brothel. The Stafflebacks figured that there was no sin in killing men who were going to hand over their hard-earned money to prostitutes, and so with a certain smugness they dispatched the wicked miscreants as swiftly as they could.

The gangs of New York City among others

The spirit of the lawless West continued into the 20th century with the public enemies of the Prohibition era, among whom were Ma Barker and her 'boys'. Kate Barker and her sons were accused of carrying out a campaign of kidnapping and armed robberies during the early 1930s, which led to J. Edgar Hoover calling Ma Barker 'the most vicious, dangerous and resourceful criminal brain of the last decade'. However, this may have been a cynical attempt by the FBI director to justify the killing of an old woman who may not have planned or participated in the crimes after all.

The days of the outlaws were numbered after Prohibition was repealed in December 1933 and the FBI were granted permission to pursue all bank robbers and other gangsters across state lines, but soon organized crime became the business of Italian-American crime families. The Mafia families had their roots in the Sicilian Cosa Nostra and its southern Italian rivals – the Camorra from Naples and the 'Ndranghetta from Calabria. The 'made men' (fully initiated members) of the Mafia were all related by blood and had sworn to 'omertà', the vow of silence which protected 'the brotherhood' from betrayal. This repeatedly defeated all attempts to destroy the Mafia's insidious influence and addiction to violence by planting informers in its midst or turning family members against their own.

Though the Mafia no longer has a visible presence on the streets of American cities, the Godfathers of New York's five crime families have come a long way from the backstreet hoods who formed the Black Hand extortion and bootlegging gangs. But while they may now portray themselves as 'legitimate' businessmen they are far from 'untouchable', as several high-profile cases have proven. Nor are the blood ties that once held the five families together any guarantee of filial loyalty.

Aged Sicilian gangster Charles 'Lucky' Luciano limps down a street on his native island in 1949 followed by a couple of cheeky kids imitating him. He had returned from prison in America, where he had been instrumental in legitimizing organized crime.

Aberrant behaviour

Crime families, specifically those engaged in organized crime, have made a conscious choice to pursue illegal activities primarily for profit, but what of those families whose members qualify as 'evil' by virtue of barbarity for its own sake? Some are so dysfunctional and messed up that they turn in on themselves and mete out cruelty to their own family members.

Fred and Rosemary West are one of the most notorious and well-documented examples, but there are numerous other cases which suggest that such aberrant behaviour is not as uncommon as we might like to think.

In 1998, 'Fat Lucie' Lefranc was charged with keeping her husband prisoner in a rabbit hutch in his own home and forcing him to share his meals with a vicious family dog that she had trained to intimidate him. Their two eldest sons were also encouraged to rape their sister, who subsequently gave birth to six children who were then murdered and buried in the family garden.

Then in 2009 Mohammad Shafia, his wife Tooba and his son Hamed were convicted of murdering three teenage members of their own family and Shafia's first wife in what they claimed were 'honour killings', but which were revealed to be nothing more than a desperate attempt to cover up long-term abuse.

Cases such as these invariably raise questions regarding the origin of aberrant behaviour and the failings of the welfare services. But perhaps a more pertinent question to ask might be why the abusers continue to perpetrate cruelty on their own and are seemingly rarely compelled by guilt or their own consciences to confess and release their victims.

Criminologists and sociologists argue whether deviancy is the result of nature or nurture. However, it is likely that a child born into a culture of violence and cruelty will become conditioned to believe that such aberrant behaviour is not only acceptable but is also the source of parental approval.

Putting the pressure on

Most inexplicable of all are those instances in which someone with a psychopathic personality will persuade a weaker sibling or partner to participate in their homicidal activities, or a controlling parent will convince their children to join them in their killing spree, after conditioning them to share their distorted perception of the world.

In the late 1970s, when young men were succumbing in droves to *Saturday Night Fever*, the Briley brothers of Richmond, Virginia were getting their kicks from torturing and murdering their neighbours and anyone else they took a dislike to.

And in the 1980s, Utah oddball Watson Lafferty abused and brainwashed his two unbalanced sons, Dan and Ron, until they slaughtered their own sister-in-law and her teenage daughter.

Around the same time, the Bondurant brothers in Tennessee lured their victims to their sinister house, where they killed and dismembered them before burying their bodies in the grounds and earning themselves the tag 'the Evil Twins'.

In India in the 1990s the bloody trail left by the Shankar brothers revealed the tragic fate of countless young women who disappeared from their homes every day, many of them sold into prostitution by their own parents. The Shankars claimed they had kidnapped and killed the teenagers to cover up for the politicians who had raped their victims.

Also in the 1990s, former prostitute Sante Kimes and her son were living the money-grubbing creed 'greed is good'. They murdered a wealthy New York widow so they could live in her luxury apartment, Sante having squandered a considerable fortune inherited from her recently deceased millionaire husband. When questioned, the 'black widow' claimed that the former tenant had taken a prolonged vacation, but when the deception was uncovered so too was a lifetime of crime. It involved the brutal enslavement and torture of young Mexican servant girls, insurance fraud and the killing of several witnesses who could have put Sante behind bars.

More recently, the four González sisters racked up 91 verified killings at their hostelry in Mexico, earning a place in *Guinness World Records* for 'the Most Prolific Murder Partnership'.

The new millennium brought no let-up in the murderous and depraved activities of those with an insatiable lust for blood. In China, the Shen brothers frequented clubs and bars in order to prey on prostitutes, whom they butchered and ate, disposing of the unappetizing body parts by dissolving them in acid. Incredibly, they recruited several willing female accomplices, who revealed the grisly details after their arrest in 2004.

One thing leads to another

Abuse often leads to the abused perpetrating abuse themselves. Violence, too, often leads to more violence and in the past society has sought to remedy these abusive and violent acts by meting out a punishment to fit the crime.

But capital punishment has proven to be no deterrent and the catalogue of heinous crimes within the family and by 'evil' families continues to this day.

At the time of writing an unidentified German couple have been convicted of a crime which could become more common in the age

It's 1951 and Cleveland Browns owner Mickey McBride (centre) is asked to explain a murky horseracing newswire service called Continental Press to the Kefauver Committee. Keeping it all in the family, he named his son as its owner, leaving a lot of people shaking their heads. Wire services like this one allowed bookies to take bets on races where they already knew the results. It was a licence to print money.

of the internet. They were found guilty of selling their own son to paedophiles on the virtual black market known as the Dark Web.

After reading this and other disturbing cases detailed over the following pages you may agree that it is not a case of identifying the 'criminal gene' which prompts certain individuals to execute horrific crimes, but of creating a society which no longer provides a breeding ground for abuse of any kind. Until that utopia is achieved, there will be more cases to add to the lamentable catalogue of crimes detailed in this book.

No doubt many of those whose crimes are examined in the following pages would have justified their acts of theft and murder by claiming that they were only doing what was necessary to survive in a hostile and violent world. Nature is cruel, they might have argued, and they were only doing what came naturally. But if that was their initial impulse, it soon became a compulsion and a convenient excuse to do as they wished and damn the consequences.

According to John Berger (1926–2017), British essayist and author of *Ways of Seeing*: 'Nothing in the nature around us is evil. This needs to be repeated since one of the human ways of talking oneself into inhuman acts is to cite the supposed cruelty of nature.'

Chapter One:
Bloody History

Human beings have an innate capacity for cruelty, but the majority of us control our baser instincts and exhibit a desire to create or appreciate those things that enrich our lives and the world. History has recorded countless cases of tyrannical dynasties that enforced their rule with gratuitous barbarism while presiding over empires which advanced the cause of civilization and saw the creation of great works of art, the building of architectural marvels and cultural wonders which still inspire awe to this day.

Among them were the pitiless, hot-blooded Caesars of ancient Rome, who were corrupted by power and made mad by murder. They demanded public displays of gladiatorial combat and other barbaric spectacles to satiate their bloodlust and provide entertainment for their restive subjects. However, the basic principles of Roman law provided the foundation for the Western legal system and the Romans disseminated Greek culture throughout their empire as well as the civilizing influence of Christianity.

In ancient China a line of emperors, both male and female, devised ever more ingenious means of torture and ritual execution and yet also found the time to leave a legacy of art treasures, including woodblock-printed books centuries before Europe had a printing press.

Then in medieval and Tudor England a succession of kings and queens slaughtered their own family members to secure the throne, and ruled their subjects with an iron fist, while court artists and architects raised monumental cathedrals and produced splendid decorative art, including tapestries, portraits, stained glass and jewellery.

During the Italian Renaissance Machiavellian princes and vindictive noble families plotted the eradication of political and romantic rivals while Michelangelo, Leonardo da Vinci, Raphael and many other illustrious artists were producing masterpieces that demonstrated to what heights the human soul could rise.

Hail, Caesar

Citizens of Rome might boast that the claim of 'Civus romanus sum' set them apart from barbarians and slaves, and it was true up to a point, but Roman citizens lived in a society that accepted pain, cruelty, and torture as the norm, and in which there was no suggestion of equality at birth or mercy in the afterlife.

Michael Korda (1933–), English novelist

The torture of cangue or tcha in China, an illustration by Gustave Doré from 1858. The hands are tied to each arm of a yoke; it was similar to the pillory in Europe.

Legend has it that Rome was founded by murderers, thieves and runaway slaves, the latter having obtained their freedom by slaying their masters. According to Colin Wilson's authoritative *A Criminal History of Mankind*, this would explain the 'fatal deficiency' in the Roman character, an obsessive materialism, greed and acquisitiveness which resulted in the centre of the empire witnessing 'more crime and violence than any [. . .] other city in world history'. As Wilson points out, the impression one has from reading fictional novels such as Robert Graves' *I, Claudius* is that of relentless 'murder, assassination, intrigue, promiscuity and sexual perversion'.

For all its architectural and engineering feats, Rome's fortunes rose and fell under a succession of Caesars who seized and secured their rule through political murder. From the assassination of the tribune Tiberius Gracchus in 133 BC to the fall of the empire in the fifth century AD, the history of Rome is stained with blood. From that day to this, violence has served as the means for various prominent figures in Italian history – from the early popes and the ruthless heads of Renaissance families to Mafia Godfathers – to enforce their authority and eliminate their enemies.

Wilson identified the source of this lethal tradition when he wrote: 'The Romans were slipping into violence by a process of self-justification . . . once murder has been justified on the grounds of expediency, it can become a habit, then a disease.'

Claudius

One of the first of the 12 Caesars to succumb to this disorder was the deceptively benign Claudius, a man of 'cruel and sanguinary' disposition according to the Roman historian Suetonius. Claudius married his niece, Agrippina, after having the law against incest repealed but he would live to regret it. When he refused to adopt her

A bust of Claudius who is portrayed without any undue modesty as Jupiter, king of the gods.

son by a previous marriage (the infamous Nero) she poisoned him in AD 54. Contrary to the picture of the stuttering, indecisive and gentle ruler portrayed by Graves, the surviving records of imperial executions and confessions extracted under torture at the behest of Claudius suggest that he was as callous and unforgiving as his deranged nephew Caligula and his sadistic uncle Tiberius.

Claudius savoured scenes of torture and execution, the more sadistic and prolonged, the better. He particularly enjoyed watching men being whipped until the flesh was flayed from their bones and he found it amusing to send those who displeased him to their death in the arena – not to fight in gladiatorial combat but to be eaten alive by lions. Among his victims were members of his own family: the husband of his eldest daughter, the father of his son-in-law, two of his own nieces and his first wife Messalina.

Messalina was eliminated in one night's bloodbath, which saw the execution of over 300 men and women who had participated in the orgies she had organized. Claudius refused to hear the pleas of those who were accused after he learned that they had witnessed a contest between their hostess and a well-known *meretrix*, or harlot, to see who could handle the most men in one night. It would seem that even a promiscuous Roman god (Claudius had been deified during his reign) had his own peculiar sense of morality and that those who surpassed him in the sexual stakes would forfeit their life.

Nero

If the rumours circulating in Rome in AD 54 were true, the newly crowned emperor Nero may have been the consequence of an incestuous relationship between Caligula and his own sister, Agrippina the Younger. If so, this may account for his narcissistic self-absorption and the callous indifference he displayed when the capital went up in

Emperor Nero oversees the torture of Christian subjects by burning at the stake in Ancient Rome.

flames. But other than that, he accepted the symbols of power with uncharacteristic humility. His one vice appeared to be his ambition to perform on the stage and bask in the applause of an adoring audience. But within a year he had poisoned his half-brother Britannicus, whom he suspected of plotting to overthrow him. He dismissed his accusers by declaring that the son of Claudius and Messalina was an epileptic and that sudden death was inevitable. Poison would seem to have been Nero's favoured method of dispatching his enemies as he was known to find the sight of blood nauseating.

At first mother and son engaged in an aggressively competitive relationship, with Agrippina the Younger making it clear that she had the right to dominate both her son and the empire. But this soon became a more intimate contest, with mother and son indulging in an incestuous relationship until he tired of her and conspired to have her killed. However, she survived the attempt in March AD 59 and a female friend was beaten to death by mistake. On her return, Agrippina was attacked by her son's tutor and two assassins, who hacked her to death with their swords. The Roman senator and historian Tacitus described the harrowing scene in highly melodramatic terms, with the empress baring her abdomen and begging the assassins to strike the fatal blow at the womb which had borne her treacherous son.

True to character, Nero then played the victim, pretending to be the target of a failed assassination attempt orchestrated by his deranged mother, who had taken her own life when the plot was discovered. To his relief and delight, Nero discovered that his popularity had increased as a result of the failed 'plot' to assassinate him and no suspicion had attached to his name. As with his uncles and his possible father Caligula before him, he realized that the citizens of Rome were prepared to set aside any reservations they might have regarding the behaviour, and even the sanity, of their rulers, provided they were

A Roman orgy in the banquet hall of a nobleman during the golden days of 'imperial splendour'.

entertained and distracted by 'bread and circuses' – blood sports with lavish banquets laid on between spectacles.

At this point, Nero was restless for further sexual conquests and though he had his pick of both boys and young girls he perversely took a particular fancy to the wife of his close friend Otho, the pregnant Poppaea. Otho might have been persuaded to give her up (especially after he learned that Nero had seriously considered having him murdered if he did not release her), but there was another obstacle in Nero's path, his own wife Octavia. In order to obtain a divorce, the unblemished reputation of the adolescent and chaste daughter of Claudius and Messalina would have to be fatally compromised and a confession of adultery obtained by any means that her devious husband could devise.

But having obtained the necessary evidence from her slaves and servants under torture, Nero was shocked to have his will opposed by the people. The good citizens of Rome had their price, but they would evidently not be party to the false slandering of their virtuous young empress, so they gathered outside the palace and made their opposition known. It was only after one of Nero's cronies, Anicetus, falsely confessed to having fathered a child with Octavia that public support for her died away. They were promised she would not die but would be banished and she was duly transported to an island. This was sufficient to quell the unrest, but while far from Rome she was murdered and her head brought back to the capital to satisfy Poppaea.

Even an emperor can go too far

Nero was popular with the citizens of Rome until AD 64, when he initiated the persecution of an apocalyptic Jewish sect which awaited the return of their prophet, the crucified Nazarene, and the imminent end of the world. The Christians were unpopular for their

As emperor, Nero had his pick of whomsoever he fancied and he never stinted on pandering to his own perversity.

Nero surveys the city of Rome after the fire in AD *64, but did he start the blaze himself?*

fanatical zeal, but Nero mistook the public's dislike for loathing and butchered so many that both senators and citizens alike thought him excessively cruel.

What disturbed them was not only the vast number of Christians that had been put to death, but the way in which many of them met their end as martyrs. Their oppressors lacked compassion, but they were uneasy and troubled by the Christians' readiness to die for their faith. It unsettled them.

The Romans had their gods, but they were not spiritually inclined. They were by nature materialists, with little thought for the afterlife and no inclination to contemplate the purpose of existence beyond the fact that it provided an opportunity to enjoy themselves. (During Nero's reign one wealthy citizen spent four million sesterces, equivalent to $4 million (£3.1m) today, on flowers to adorn a magnificent banquet presided over by a huge statue of the emperor several storeys high.) Yet here, in their midst, were those who had nothing in the manner of material possessions, nor status, and yet they appeared to possess something that could not be seen or valued but which gave meaning to their otherwise wretched lives.

The mass crucifixions, the bloody spectacle of families being thrown to the lions and ripped apart by dogs and the burning alive of those who had been tied to posts and daubed with tar proved too much even for the usually indifferent citizens. A groundswell was building against Nero, which gathered momentum the following year when Poppaea died after being beaten by her husband while she was heavily pregnant. The elaborate funeral was seen as being as much Nero's attempt to assuage his guilt as it was an outpouring of grief and soon afterwards he brought further discredit to the title of Caesar by marrying a eunuch who was said to have castrated himself. Knowing that he could be denied nothing, he then 'married' a second male concubine, but for this ceremony he appeared as the bride and was said to have imitated the coital moans of a young girl while being sodomized by the 'groom'.

As dissent spread, the Senate members feared that they might be added to the list of conspirators that the paranoid emperor was now drawing up in the wake of a failed assassination attempt by a clique of nobles. Still afflicted with a queasy revulsion to blood, Nero ordered those he suspected of disloyalty to commit suicide by opening their veins while immersed in a hot tub. His most successful general and many senior commanders were given this option and were denied the right to contest the unfounded allegations.

One by one the governors of distant provinces denounced Nero's excesses and refused to implement his edicts or collect the punitive taxes he had recently imposed. The legions then began to defect to the rebels and one morning Nero woke to find that even his Praetorian guard had deserted him. When the news reached him that the Senate had voted unanimously for his arrest, he had hysterics and wailed: 'What a loss I shall be to the arts.' Lacking the nerve to kill himself, he had an attendant drive the sword blade home. He was the last of the hereditary Caesars.

The merciless Mings

The 16 emperors of the Ming dynasty ruled China for almost 300 years, from 1368 to 1644, and all were related by blood – the blood that coursed through their imperial veins and the blood they spilled to enforce their divine right to rule. Sons succeeded fathers and nephews succeeded their uncles. The emperor was believed to be divine and so sovereignty could only be passed to blood relatives. Each also inherited the power to impose the odious penalty known as 'nine familial exterminations', under which nine generations of a family were executed for the transgression committed by one of its members.

However, this did not satisfy the bloodlust of the first of the Ming emperors, Hongwu, a former military commander who seized the throne as his reward for having driven the Mongols out of China in 1368. When he learned that his chief minister was conspiring against him, he ordered the execution of everyone who was known to associate with the accused. Friends, family members, distant relatives, associates and acquaintances were all slaughtered – 40,000 people in total.

And the methods of execution were devised to maximize the pain and prolong suffering. Many victims were flayed alive and their skin displayed where it would serve as a deterrent to others who might be thinking of conspiring against the emperor. Hongwu also approved of the method known as 'death by a thousand cuts', under which the condemned person was hacked to pieces, one portion at a time – fingers, toes, ears, nose, limbs – each part was severed in specific order, so as to keep the prisoner conscious until the fatal blow.

Yongle

When Yongle succeeded to the throne in 1402 he increased the execution procedure to 'death by 3,000 cuts', a ritualized butchery which prolonged death by several days. Such callousness would not have lost Yongle any sleep, for he had ordered his own nephew, Jianwen (the second Ming emperor), to be burned alive inside his palace.

In its place Yongle ordered the construction of the Forbidden City, the largest palace in the world, comprising 9,000 rooms on a 180-acre site in Beijing. A million subjects were forced to work on this wonder of the ancient world, toiling as slaves for 15 years during which an unknown number died of overwork, starvation and maltreatment.

The Forbidden City in Beijing was begun during the Ming dynasty, c.1420.

His own loyal courtiers were treated no better if they were thought to have disrespected him by failing to 'kow-tow' (a formal bow to acknowledge the presence of a 'Son of Heaven'). Ironically, this custom became a crime punishable by death when the 10th Ming emperor, Zhengde, succeeded to the throne in 1505. Zhengde was so bored with palace life that he had taken a fancy to playing the role of an ordinary citizen and had a market square built in the palace grounds. He indulged in a pretence of dressing as a commoner and had his courtiers exchange their official robes for the garb of merchants and market tradesmen.

When the volatile and vindictive emperor Yongle believed himself to have been offended, even his concubines were put to death. In 1421 he had all of his 2,800 concubines slaughtered by the palace guards when he learned that one of them had committed suicide after admitting she had slept with a eunuch. Such forbidden relations were not unknown as many members of the emperor's harem were starved of affection and sought comfort in the arms of their guards. The girls had been abducted on the emperor's orders and were imprisoned in the palace, their fate dependent on the whim of their divine lord and master.

Joining their master in death

Three years later his baleful influence reached out from beyond the grave. That summer he died and according to custom his surviving concubines were formally presented with a square of red silk, symbolic of the emperor's wish that they should follow him to paradise, where they would continue to serve him. They were then ushered under guard into the great hall of the palace where a banquet awaited them, a traditional last meal comprising rare delicacies such as the ovaries of white mares and fried donkey genitals. A foreign

The emperor Yongle, who reigned from 1402 until 1424.

dignitary who witnessed the ceremony described the harrowing scene as the weeping women were forced to put the silk nooses around their necks and climb on to wooden platforms that served as scaffolds. Although ritual suicide was intended to honour their dead master, it's unlikely that their tears were shed for the man who had ordered their death.

Tragically, such sights were not a unique event, nor were they just an example of Yongle's merciless reign. His predecessors and successors demanded the same sacrifice, although the method differed. Some decreed that their concubines set themselves alight and others insisted that the young girls join them in their tomb, to be buried alive with their other chattels and treasures.

The end of a dynasty

The 11th Ming emperor Jiajing proved to be as mad and debauched as his predecessors. He was not satisfied with being worshipped as a 'Son of Heaven'. Seeking true immortality, he commanded his officials to abduct thousands of virgins so that he could bathe in their menstrual blood in the belief that it would bring him eternal life. In 1542, a group of them decided that he shouldn't be allowed to live another day and tried to strangle him while he slept, using the ribbons from their hair. But the ribbons were too thin and he woke up unharmed. Incensed, he ordered their immediate execution and that of their families.

He survived to reign for 46 years but Wanli, the 13th emperor, outlived him. In fact, Wanli was the longest-reigning emperor in the Ming dynasty, despite the fact that he was morbidly obese. Wanli satiated his sexual appetite as much as Jiajing, but he was equally fond of food and frequently devoured the lion's share of a banquet consisting of up to 100 dishes.

Long before his death in 1620 he had also squandered twice the state's annual income by constructing an imposing mausoleum for himself. Four years later, rebel armies, goaded by centuries of tyranny, descended on Beijing and chased the last Ming emperor from his palace. The 16th emperor, Chongzhen, hanged himself for shame, thereby bringing the reign of the 'Sons of Heaven' to a fittingly violent end.

The Borgias – the Devil's dynasty

> Pope Alexander VI could not avoid domestic misfortunes which perturbed his house with tragic examples and lust and horrible cruelty beyond that of all barbarous nations . . . the Cardinal of Valencia, not being able to tolerate that this position should be held by his brother, and furthermore envious that Gandia occupied a greater place than himself in the love of Madonna Lucrezia, their common sister, enflamed with lust and ambition . . . had him killed and secretly cast into the Tiber. It was equally rumoured that not only the two brothers, but the father himself, competed for the love of Madonna Lucrezia.
>
> *Francesco Guicciardini,* The History of Italy *(1532)*

Ask anyone to name the most evil family in history and many will nominate the Borgias. Their name has become synonymous with murder, intrigue, sexual depravity and corruption: an image and reputation perpetuated by countless books, paintings, plays, films and, most recently, the salacious historical TV series of the same name. But were they truly as wicked as they have been painted?

According to Johann Burchard, papal Master of Ceremonies from 1483 to 1506: 'There is no longer any crime or shameful act that does not take place in public in Rome and in the home of the Pontiff . . . monstrous acts of lechery . . . rapes and acts of incest are countless . . . throngs of courtesans throng St Peter's Palace, pimps, brothels and whorehouses are to be found everywhere!'

Rodrigo de Borja, who took the title Pope Alexander VI, was accused of having bought the papacy in 1492 purely for the power it conferred upon him. His subsequent depravity led a Venetian diplomat to declare that Satan's servant was now enthroned in the Vatican. In the weeks that followed Alexander's death in August 1503, the Marquess of Mantua wrote to his wife of the rumours that were already circulating. It was said that Alexander had sold his soul for the papacy and that seven demons had been seen around his death bed, while his body 'began to boil and his mouth to foam like a cauldron upon a fire'.

The origin of this legend may have arisen from the state of the Pope's corpse, which was on public display in the sweltering summer heat. In the words of an eyewitness of the time:

> It was a revolting scene to look at that deformed, blackened corpse, prodigiously swelled, and exhaling an infectious smell; his lips and nose were covered with brown drivel, his mouth was opened very widely . . . therefore no fanatic or devotee dared to kiss his feet or hands, as custom would have required.

The news of Alexander's death was said to have been greeted with great relief and rejoicing in the streets of the capital. In his *History of Italy*, Guicciardini wrote:

All Rome thronged with incredible rejoicing to see the dead body of Alexander in Saint Peter's, unable to satiate their eyes enough with seeing that serpent who in his boundless ambition and pestiferous perfidy, and with all his examples of horrible cruelty and monstrous sensuality and unheard-of avarice . . .

Family roots

Rodrigo's uncle, Alfons de Borja, had accumulated the fortune on which the dynasty was founded and with which his descendants bribed their way to power and paid their assassins to eliminate their enemies. Alfons had incurred the condemnation of his cronies and confidants for the flagrant corruption that characterized his reign as Pope Calixtus III, but his sins were surpassed by those of Alexander's offspring, whom Burchard described as 'utterly depraved'. (Alexander fathered eight children with at least three different women.)

Pope Alexander's daughter, Lucrezia (1480–1519), was accused of being a whore, a witch and a poisoner. She was also widely believed to have had an incestuous relationship with her father. Her brother Cesare (1475–1507) was also said to have slept with her and to have murdered his own brother, Juan. But as Cesare's power was considerably diminished when he relinquished the role of cardinal to assume his dead brother's duties, it is more likely that Juan's killer was Cardinal Sforza, a sworn enemy of the Borgias and the man who had the most to gain from Juan's death.

A hell of a party

But perhaps the most persistent stain on the family is the notorious all-night orgy in the papal palace, at which the guests, including

Lucrezia Borgia was accused of being a whore, a witch and a poisoner. It was also said she had slept with her father and her brother Cesare.

senior officials of the Church, were attended and entertained by 50 of the most expensive harlots in Rome. It became known as 'the Banquet of the Chestnuts' because the prostitutes were encouraged by the lecherous guests to pick up scattered chestnuts without using their fingers, feet or mouths. After the game, their papal host presided over a mass orgy in which the male with the greatest number of satisfied partners was declared the winner and was rewarded with costly finery. Alexander VI was not the first nor the last pope to use the Vatican for lewd purposes, but it appears that he was unwise enough to choose a sacred religious holiday (30 October) for his pagan bacchanalia.

However, the almost certainly fictitious episode could have been the creation of the family's severest critic, Johann Burchard, who disapproved of the Borgias' pivotal role in Vatican politics and their selling of religious favours and papal offices. Burchard was merely voicing the disapproval shared by many who deplored Alexander VI's blatant nepotism. Ten of his relatives had been admitted to the College of Cardinals and titles, land and unmerited authority were bestowed on many more of his relatives and cronies in the papal states.

It is always possible that some of the crimes of which the Borgias were accused were no more than malicious gossip and that the primary source of their purported crimes was an anonymous letter sent to Silvio Savelli, a military commander, accusing Alexander and his sons of an incestuous relationship with Lucrezia – an accusation which was not taken too seriously at the time.

The Black Legend

Documents recently discovered in the Vatican archive reveal that many of the slurs and accusations originated with rival families, who were jealous of the Borgia's power and influence and were also contemptuous of their origins. The Borgias were of Spanish stock (their original name being de Borja) and that made them 'outsiders' as far as Rome's nobility were concerned. Rome's aristocracy would not countenance such 'upstarts' attaining status in what Machiavelli called the *alti luoghi* (high places) of Italian society and despised all those who appeared to be enriching themselves at the expense of Italian nobles. Italy was then infected with a virulent hatred of Spain known as the 'Black Legend', which promoted the myth that all Spaniards were cruel, rapacious and barbarous. They saw the Borgias as despicable infiltrators who were indecently impatient for power and status.

One of the most persistent myths surrounding the family is that Cesare murdered his sister's lover in the sight of his father, Pope Alexander VI. It was a story disseminated by the Venetian ambassador at a time when Venice was an enemy of Rome. By comparison with his contemporaries, Cesare was a model of restraint, executing only those he knew to be conspiring against him.

Even Machiavelli, the political philosopher and prince of foxes, put in a favourable mention of Cesare in his memoirs. He wrote:

> I think I have been right in putting him forward as an example for all those who have acquired power through good fortune and the arms of others. He was a man of great courage and high intentions, and he could not have conducted himself other than the way he did; his plans were frustrated only because Alexander's life was cut short and because of his own sickness.

It appears in the end that Lucrezia might have been merely a schemer and arch-manipulator of men, but not the witch she was painted to be, for her death in childbirth was widely mourned. Her reputation was blackened by her embittered first husband, Giovanni Sforza, who

Cesare Borgia – did he murder his sister's lover in front of his father, Pope Alexander VI?

resented the dissolution of their marriage by her interfering father, Pope Alexander VI. Lucrezia's use of poison, if true, was not peculiar to her as it was the customary means of murder in Renaissance Italy. But this too could have been yet another attempt to vilify the family.

Lucrezia, it seems, was an intelligent and cultured woman and a capable manager of her father's office and her third husband's estates. It was her refined sensibilities and passion for the arts that captured the heart of the poet Pietro Bembo, with whom she had a short love affair and a lifelong friendship. The former lovers maintained an affectionate correspondence for 16 years until Lucrezia's death, penning what Lord Byron would later call: 'The prettiest love letters in the world.' (The poet was forbidden to copy the letters but managed to steal a lock of Lucrezia's hair from the Ambrosiana Library in Milan, where the letters were stored.)

Bembo counted the painter Raphael among his friends and was painted in his youth by Bellini and in old age by Titian. It seems unlikely that a man of such refinement would be a lover and a lifelong friend of Lucrezia Borgia if she was indeed a whore, a witch and a habitual poisoner.

It would appear then that the Borgias were not entirely evil but ruthlessly ambitious and were no doubt cold-blooded when it came to dispatching political rivals. However, they were probably no more so than the Medici family in Florence, the Malatesta in Rimini and the Sforza in Milan, but those who maligned them did it so effectively that the Borgia name remains a byword in evil to this day.

Chapter Two:
Bred in the Bone

All in the family

In Scotland during the 15th century there were no state benefits to feed and clothe the unemployed and no subsidized housing to accommodate the homeless. So when the itinerant tanner Sawney Beane set up home with his young bride in Ballantrae, Ayrshire they considered themselves fortunate to find a cave that offered more than shelter from the harsh Scottish winter.

The location was fortuitous for Sawney, who soon discovered that the cave at Bennane Head on Scotland's west coast was situated on a route used by travellers and merchants. They could be lured into the cave with the promise of shelter and then be robbed and murdered, unheard and unseen by the local villagers.

Although there was no organized law enforcement to hinder his homicidal activities, Sawney risked summary execution by a mob of incensed locals if his crimes were discovered, so he had to find a way to dispose of the bodies. Whether he was driven to cannibalism by starvation or a taste for human flesh is not known, but by chopping up and cooking his victims he fed his growing family and rid himself of the evidence at a stroke. The victims' clothes and other belongings provided all the growing clan needed, thus saving them from having to visit the nearest villages, where they risked arousing the curiosity of the inhabitants.

Caught in the act

Over the course of 25 years Mrs Beane produced a prodigious brood of little Beanes – 14 in total – all of whom needed clothing and feeding. They in turn began interbreeding, but the cave was more than adequate to accommodate the extended family. A labyrinth of tunnels, some of which were a mile long, provided them with a home and a hiding place while they racked up more murders than could be accounted for by highwaymen and wild beasts. Aided by his growing brood, Sawney was able to ambush and murder several travellers at a time.

However, when salted, decomposing body parts began to be washed up on a nearby shoreline the authorities were forced to act. They sent out search parties, but at first they couldn't find the missing parts that might have helped identify the victims. And they did not think to explore the Beanes' cave because its entrance was flooded at

Alexander Beane, aka Sawney, lived in a cave in south Ayrshire with his family; he and his close relatives were said to have killed and eaten passers-by.

high tide, making it an unlikely habitat for ordinary folks but a perfect hiding place for felons.

It was only by a stroke of good fortune that the perpetrators were finally tracked down and brought to justice. When they attacked a man and his wife on horseback, the husband managed to fend them off until a large group of locals returning from a fair arrived on the scene. A brutal hand-to-hand struggle ensued and for once the clan found themselves outnumbered. They beat a hasty retreat, only to be pursued by an angry mob intent on avenging the murdered wife who had been butchered before she could be rescued. Although Sawney and his 'army' evaded their pursuers, there were now living witnesses to their crimes and many brutal murders to be avenged.

Savage justice

The chief magistrate of Glasgow considered the matter sufficiently serious to justify appealing to the king for assistance and soon 400 soldiers were scouring the countryside, assisted by bloodhounds. It was the dogs who led the king's men to the flooded cave at Bennane Head. The stench of human flesh was so strong that the dogs could smell it, even though the pickled body parts were stored deep inside the cave where the troops were to find piles of discarded clothes, rings and other valuables belonging to the victims. The 48-strong Beane clan was no match for King James's troops and after a brief skirmish the family members were arrested and brought to Edinburgh for trial.

Each one of them was sentenced to death and butchered in public with the same savagery the clan had meted out to their victims. But these were brutal, pitiless times and justice had to be seen to be carried out without mercy as a lesson to others. The men had their limbs cut off and slowly bled to death and then the women were burned alive.

Four hundred of the king's men scoured the rugged Scottish countryside hunting for the Beane family.

It was savage justice, but no mercy had been shown to those who had died at the hands of Beane and his brood.

A curious postscript states that there was a lone survivor of the skirmish in the cave – a young girl of 17 who was taken in by a local family who were also in the habit of killing and eating stray travellers. She subsequently married their son and gave birth to a boy, but being a mother did not merit any consideration from the law and she was still hanged. Her husband and son were said to have escaped to the New World, where they established a colony on Roanoke Island, North Carolina, the legendary 'lost colony' whose inhabitants mysteriously disappeared shortly after their arrival in 1587.

The Kansas cannibals

It is possible, but of course unlikely, that Sawney Beane's descendants could have been responsible for the spate of cannibal killings in Labette County, Kansas in the 1870s, specifically those descended from the 17-year-old female who survived the skirmish in the cave at Bennane Head. But it's more likely wishful thinking on the part of those who would like to find a link between the two murderous families.

The Bender 'family' were thought to be German immigrants who spoke little English and relied on their young daughter Kate to lure travellers to their ramshackle inn just off the Osage Mission wagon trail, north-east of Cherryvale. But Kate and her 'brother' John, a simple-minded hayseed with a wide-eyed stare and a habit of laughing inanely at his own foolishness, may not have been blood relations after all. It was believed by some that John Bender Jnr was born John Gebhardt and that he and his 'sister' Kate were living as husband and wife. Another story has it that they were in the habit of killing their own children to avoid evidence of their 'incestuous' relationship.

Kate, who was then in her early twenties, loitered at the side of the road engaging in conversation with weary travellers. She assured them that they would be better off for a warm bed and a meal at the family inn. Kate claimed to possess psychic abilities and would perform a sham clairvoyant act to ensnare the paying guests into sitting in a seat reserved for the family's victims. She would then find out everything she could about the potential victims, to be certain that no one would come looking for them and to discover if they were carrying anything that might be valuable. Meanwhile, her brother John would be looking through the victims' wagons or saddlebags to see if there was anything worth murdering them for. The Benders saw no purpose in killing if they couldn't show a profit.

Distracted by Kate's sham fortune-telling, they did not see or hear her father emerge from behind a curtain with a six-pound collier's hammer in his hand.

The victims had their skulls crushed and Kate would then slit their throats just to be sure. Then their bodies were stripped of clothes and valuables and dropped through a trapdoor under the table into a six-foot square pit. A tunnel led to the back of the house, where the bodies could be dragged before being buried nearby.

Gruesome discoveries

One man and his companion escaped with their lives after they refused to sit in the 'place of honour'. Their refusal aroused Ma Bender's ire and the potential victims became suspicious. When her husband and son emerged from behind the curtain with murder in their eyes, the two men made their excuses and left.

The recent unexplained disappearance of a popular local doctor then aroused the curiosity of the authorities, who held a public meeting in spring 1873 to determine what to do next. It was agreed

1. Grave of Dr. York. 2. Grave of M'Kenzie. 3. Grave of M'Croatly. 4. Grave of Brown. 5. Grave of unknown. 6. Grave of unknown. 7. Grave of Longcors and child. 8. Pit or cellar in which bodies were cast.

SCENE OF THE BENDER MURDERS.—[FROM A SKETCH BY JOHN W. DONLADY.]

The scene of the Benders' murders from a sketch by John W. Donlady, with at least seven graves marked and featuring the pit near the barn where the bodies were dumped.

that a search party would be formed and all homes in the area would be searched. But the Benders were also at that meeting and when the search party arrived at their clapboard hostelry, they were nowhere to be found.

However, they had left in such haste that they hadn't bothered to erase the evidence of their crimes. The stench of congealed blood led the search party to the trapdoor and down into the cellar, where they discovered traces of human remains. Outside, in a corner of the orchard, they dug up nine bodies including that of the missing doctor, all deposited in unmarked shallow graves. As the news of the gruesome discoveries spread, a large crowd of onlookers gathered at the site. This attracted the attention of a local photographer, Julius Pleetz, from nearby Independence, who recorded the grisly scene for posterity. A post-mortem revealed that among the bodies were those of children and an infant who had been buried alive.

They found the fatal knife hidden in a clock in the kitchen and three hammers, but no trace of the family. During the search, souvenir hunters took the opportunity to strip the inn of clapboard, some stones from the cellar, the painted sign which hung on the outside offering 'Groceries' and even splinters from the fence, leaving nothing but a hole in the ground where the inn had once stood.

Continuing fascination

There are those who insist that the law never caught up with the Benders, though members of several posses claimed to have killed one or more of the family as they attempted to evade justice. Whatever the truth, their crimes continued to exert a morbid fascination and in the 1970s a local museum erected a reconstruction of their home. A highway marker was also raised, to mark the spot where the killings had taken place. There were even rumours that film director

Guillermo del Toro was seriously considering adapting their story for a big budget horror movie, though it came to nothing.

The Bender case could be filed away as the story of yet another family of homicidal hicks in the backwoods were it not for the fact that Kate Bender's behaviour suggests there was something more interesting in the mix. According to the legend, Kate was no beauty but a tall, gawky, bow-legged girl with a prominent squint. Others describe her as 'a mighty good looker' and 'strikingly beautiful but Satanic', with copper-coloured hair and hazel eyes. A contemporary photograph suggests that her appearance fell somewhere in between these two extremes. She was slender, buxom and 5ft 6in tall and affected an affable charm until she had her prey where she wanted them.

But she also went to great lengths to pose as a respectable member of the community. Kate and John Jnr went dutifully to Sunday school and later to church, where she became a regular member of the congregation. She also attended religious 'meetings' at the Harmony Grove schoolhouse, took singing lessons, danced at social gatherings and laughed freely. But it was all an act. She craved attention almost as much as she desired respectability and money.

Con artist?

Kate gave lectures advocating free love, which provoked condemnation from some members of her congregation but made her popular with the red-blooded men of Cherryvale. She charmed the women, too, by telling fortunes, selling curses and spells and locating lost valuables for a fee. Her desire for attention led her to falsely claim to possess qualifications she was not entitled to and to possess psychic abilities, with which she fleeced the gullible during her weekly seances.

Proclaiming herself 'Professor Miss Kate Bender', she posted bills throughout the county advertising love potions and quack cures 'for all sorts of diseases, blindness, fits, deafness and all such diseases. Also deaf and dumbness.' Such 'snake oil salesmen' and even women were a common sight in the Old West, but they were usually part of a travelling medicine show, so they could be miles away by the time their customers realized they had been duped into buying coloured water and potentially fatal mixtures. But 'Professor Kate' was sure that her victims were too stupid to realize they had been conned. Her arrogance and contempt led her to rebuff accusations that she was a con artist and she brazened it out until the sickening truth about her family inevitably emerged with the discovery of the bodies at the family roadhouse.

Grisly escape method

Almost every sensational murder case generates its own mythology and the Bender killings produced their share. One hoary tale doing the rounds well into the 1950s had it that the local sheriff decided to investigate the murders by pretending to be drunk and then allowing Kate to seduce him. The sheriff thought he could handle the Benders single-handed, but as soon as Kate took him into the back room he was overpowered and killed. In the struggle he managed to get off a single shot, which hit Kate Bender right between the eyes. The next day the townspeople found the two bodies but there was no sign of Ma and Pa Bender, nor of Kate's brother John Jnr.

It was believed by some that John Snr, Kate's father, had escaped to Idaho, where he was given food and shelter by a good Samaritan who had no idea who he was helping. The kindly old man was then killed by Bender, who stole his horse. As the old expression goes, 'No good deed goes unpunished'.

John Bender was described as a 'wild woolly man' and 'a gorilla', with black piercing eyes and thick bushy eyebrows. His real name was

John Flickinger and he stood over six feet tall, with broad shoulders and powerful arms that could crush a weaker man. He was said to have a permanent sullen, distrustful expression and rarely looked any of his neighbours in the eye. Like his wife, he spoke little English and when he did his speech was peppered with colourful expletives.

Some people said that a local posse captured the fugitive and brought him back to the town of Salmon for trial and a swift lynching, but once they learned his identity some were eager to take him back to Kansas and collect the reward money. While they argued among themselves, Bender managed to escape by sawing off his foot with a pocket knife, but he died from loss of blood before he could get more than a couple of miles.

Determined not to be cheated out of the reward, the townspeople attempted to preserve the body by burying it in a swamp until the weather turned cold enough to transport it. But while they waited the corpse was stolen by a native American, who decapitated it and boiled the head so that he would have a skull to offer to his gods. It was later retrieved and put on display in a saloon, where the customers could gawk in wonder at the head of John Bender and brood on the fate of those who commit the ultimate sin, taking another person's life.

More prosaically, others said he was murdered in 1884 by his wife and daughter, who were bent on revenge after he abandoned them to their fate and fled with the proceeds of their crimes.

Ma Bender and Kate go free

The fate of John Jnr is also uncertain, although it is said that he died of a stroke after a long manhunt had forced him to seek sanctuary in the badlands of Texas or Mexico.

According to the account published in *The Benders of Kansas* (1913), written by defence attorney John Towner James, who took part in the trial of Kate and her mother in May 1890, both women had been accused of killing Dr William York, the local physician, whose body was the only one to be formally identified and named on the arrest warrant. Incredibly, though, the two women were released shortly after their arrest in February because the county did not want the expense of having to feed and guard the prisoners during the three months until the trial could be held.

Ma Bender was described by James as being a heavy-set woman of 55 with a marked stoop and an indomitable will. Her heavy-lidded eyes were penetrating and she possessed a vicious temper, leading her neighbours to describe her as a 'she-devil'. 'If we thought Mr Bender was an ugly cuss,' one of them remarked, 'she's no improvement.' Her menfolk feared her and did not dare to stand up to her.

She had been born Almira Meik and had previously been married to a man to whom she had borne a dozen children. He died shortly after she had given birth to their youngest child, the cause of death being a hammer blow to the head. Almira married again – more than once – and each of her husbands met the same fate. Her vicious nature allowed her to show no pity, even for her own children – three of them were believed to have been murdered to prevent them from testifying against their own kith and kin. Kate was thought to be her fifth child and she survived because she sided with her mother and shared the old woman's craving for blood.

The Kelly family

The year 1888 was a vintage year for serial killers. In Victorian London the Whitechapel murders were being blamed on an elusive figure the press had dubbed Jack the Ripper, while on the other side of the Atlantic yet another homicidal family had been arrested and were facing the swift and brutal justice meted out to murderers in the lawless West.

On 21 January 1888 the *National Police Gazette* reported the lynching of four 'foul wretches' and posed the question: 'Are they the Benders?' It was a reasonable assumption, for the similarities between the two families were quite extraordinary. William Kelly, his wife Kate and their adult offspring Bill and Kit were all about the same age as the Benders, though the son claimed to be just 20 and the daughter 18. And their ranch was also in Kansas.

News of their crimes spread across the state. With grim satisfaction, a Texas newspaper reported:

> the last act in one of the bloodiest of tragedies has closed, and the Kelly family have quickly met the vengeance they deserved. Two or three weeks ago the whole country was startled by a report of wholesale butchery and robbery near Oak City, in 'No Man's Land,' said to have been committed by the Kelly family who lived in a dwelling frequented by travellers.

The family did a bunk in the middle of the night when they learned they were under suspicion and were to be questioned about the disappearance of a number of travellers who were last seen asking for rooms and board at their property.

When the law showed up, there was no sign of the Kelly family anywhere, but the remains of ten of their victims were uncovered during the search.

Six bodies were found in the cellar and four more were buried in the stable. The murder weapon was then discovered at the scene, an axe still matted with blood, hair and human skin.

A posse was immediately organized and it set off in pursuit of the killers. One of the victims was subsequently identified as being a middle-aged woman, while the others were cattlemen who had come to Oak City to sell their herds and consequently were carrying large sums of money. Needless to say, not a dollar was found on the bodies.

Lynched by posse

The Kelly family had ridden through nearby Beaver City the day after they abandoned their home and were seen to have plenty of cash. They were riding on a wagon pulled by a pair of horses, with four more to spare, which were no doubt those belonging to the slaughtered cattlemen. As soon as the fugitives spotted the posse they abandoned the wagon and each took one of the spare horses and tried to outrun the pursuers. After a two-hour chase, three of the family were captured and only Old Man Kelly managed to escape. Kit protested her innocence, but her brother told her to accept her fate.

'It isn't any use Kit,' he told her. 'You know you had just as much to do about it as I.'

When the nooses were put around their necks, Kit asked Bill if she should confess and he replied that the lynch mob would have to find out for themselves. A moment later they were both dangling in mid-air. Their bodies were left where they died while the posse rode on after Old Man Kelly, but it was another three hours before they finally ran him to ground. By that time his horse was exhausted and the posse was close enough to fire and convince him that the game was up.

According to the newspaper report he then made a brief confession in a quiet subdued voice before he too was hanged from the nearest tree.

I moved to Kansas from the mountains of Pennsylvania
in 1869 and lived at different points along the southern

Justice could be delivered swiftly in the old Wild West, but those who administered it weren't always too concerned with the legal niceties.

border until I decided to move to No Man's Land, settled 25 miles from Beaver City and went into the cattle business. Soon after I opened a sort of tavern. Several persons disappeared while passing along this trail but as to their death I have nothing to say. A good deal of talk of foul play was made and I determined to move on to south Texas. This is all I have to say.

Perhaps he had been hoping that they might take him back to town to stand trial and that he may be able to persuade a jury there was insufficient evidence to convict him, but the posse had no doubt as to his guilt and strung him up without another word. However, they must have wanted to be sure that they would not have an innocent man's blood on their hands because they let him down and gave him one last chance to confess. He then did so, admitting that the entire family had participated in the murders of nine men and two women. After that, he also revealed where the money was hidden and gave up what he had on him, which included a gold watch engraved with the initials of one of the victims, whose body had been found at the family home. He was then hanged a second time.

A graphic illustration of the sordid event appeared across two pages in the *National Police Gazette*, with the caption: 'How Wholesale Murder Is Avenged in the Wild West. The notorious Kelly family of assassins meet with a fearful and swift doom at the hand of a furious band of cattlemen in No Man's Country.'

The Stafflebacks

There must have been something in the water in Kansas back then because the state produced a third homicidal household, the

The Stafflebacks started bumping off customers of a local brothel.

Stafflebacks, who disposed of 50 strangers, all of them customers of a local brothel. The Stafflebacks figured that there was nothing wrong in killing men who were going to give their hard-earned money to prostitutes and so they dispatched the sinners as swiftly as they could.

A report in the *Holbrook Argus*, dated November 1897, described the family as 'loathsome' and speculated that the mother, Nancy, her four children and her daughter-in-law...

> trafficked in every crime and vice from thievery to butchery, and two of whom, at least, will spend the remainder of their lives in prison. George and Ed Staffleback have been found guilty of murder in the first degree and sentenced to the penitentiary for life, while the mother, hoary in crime as in years – she is now 65 – has been found guilty of murder in the second degree and will no doubt end her years in prison, having received a twenty-five-year sentence.

The paper speculated that the source of her criminality and that of her 13 children could be traced to her 'Wyandotte Indian blood', but her first husband 'was charged by his wife and some of his children with unmentionable crimes, and the husband accused the wife of crimes equally revolting to both moral and natural laws'. So their offspring had inherited 'bad blood' on both sides and were evidently raised to believe that they could steal whatever they pleased and flout the law.

They gravitated towards the lawless side of town, specifically the aptly named Swindle Hill in Jasper County, 'a fit abode for such characters' according to the local paper.

Here congregated the degraded of both sexes, women who had forgotten the meaning of decency and men who were practiced in every crime. A man's life was not safe in the place after dark and policemen never ventured into it singly. Here the Stafflebacks lived several years, the sons practicing thievery and other crimes, for which some of them received sentences in jail, and the girls consorting with the degraded of both sexes.

It is believed that they committed their first murder there, for which two of the sons, George and Ed, were sent to prison.

Move to 'hot bed of crime'

Three years before the events that led to their final court appearance, the family moved to another 'hot bed of crime', Picker's Point on the outskirts of the town of Galena. This 'unsavoury' place had been the site of lead and zinc mining as the *Argus* continued.

Here vice reaches a depth that decency dare not attempt to describe. Rough miners, many of them foreigners, frequent the hovels and gamble and drink and swear. Ribald revelry is often interrupted by a fight that ends in murder. Then the shafts, the silent, yawning pits of the ground, are charged with another victim, which they receive into their dark depths never to yield again. If these shafts were to-day made to give up their ghastly tenants fully fifty undiscovered murders would be revealed.

Given away by floating corpse

By this point their shack was home to sons Ed, George, Mike, their sisters Louisa and Emma and George's wife Cora, all whipped into line by Nancy. The Stafflebacks had by this time acquired a reputation as a notorious and violent gang, their numbers swollen by Nancy's common law husband Charles Wilson and two young women of dubious repute, Rosa Bayne and Anna McComb. They might have continued to live unmolested by the law had Nancy not quarrelled with a miner, Frank Galbraith, whose murder 'brought the Stafflebacks to grief'. Anna McComb told the paper she had witnessed the killing.

> I heard the row begin and stepped outside and around the corner of the log hut. The old woman grabbed her corn knife and ran Galbraith out of the house. Then Wilson and Ed got their guns and began shooting at Galbraith, who started to run down the road. Wilson fired first, but missed. Then Ed fired, and I could tell that he hit him, for Frank put his hand to his hip and fell. But he got right up again and ran on. He couldn't run very fast, and Ed ran alongside of him, put his gun to his head and fired. Frank threw his hand up to his head and fell by the side of the road. Ed took the knife from the old woman and started to finish Frank by cutting his throat. All this time me and Cora had been running along after them. I grabbed Ed by the arm and begged him not to do it. 'Let me alone, or I'll slit your throat,' he said. Then he turned and cut Galbraith's throat. The blood spurted out. The old woman took the knife and wiped it on her apron.

I felt sick and me and Cora lay down in the weeds so that we could see them and they couldn't see us. They thought we had gone to the house. I was afraid to look until Cora whispered 'They're pulling his clothes off.' Then I looked. I saw Ed take him by the shoulders, and George took one leg and Wilson the other. They carried him to the old shaft and threw him in.

The corpse didn't stay down, however, and it was spotted bobbing up and down in the waterlogged shaft sometime later. Ed and George were arrested, but Wilson had skedaddled. The case against the family was sealed when Cora and Rosa turned against the rest of the bunch in an effort to save their own skins.

They revealed details of earlier murders of which the authorities had no knowledge, specifically the killing of two girls who had been living with them and who had been victims of Mike's volatile temper. After he had beaten the first girl insensible, his brother Ed murdered the other girl to keep her from snitching. Their bodies were also disposed of down the abandoned mine shaft. Other victims included a peddler who had been killed and robbed of the little money he had after being given shelter.

Nancy Staffleback died in prison in 1909, with her husband and one of her sons at her bedside dressed in their prison uniforms. It was a scene that would have moved the highly moral Victorians to tears.

Olga and Ivanova Tamarin

Ivanova Tamarin used her teenage daughter Olga to entice unsuspecting men to their deaths in her home in Estonia in the years preceding the First World War. Her arrest in July 1912 resulted in the discovery of the remains of 27 victims. The missing parts of these unfortunate men had been consumed by the two women.

Serial killers were a rarity at that time and the news of the St Petersburg 'ogress' was considered worth a few column inches in *The San Francisco Call*, which described the discovery of the mutilated bodies as a 'clew to bloody carnival of murder'. The two women had reputedly 'decoyed' both men and women to their home, which was fitted with a trapdoor leading to the cellar where the victims were imprisoned, tied and bound so they were entirely at the mercy of their sadistic captors. Valuables belonging to the victims were found in the house along with implements of torture.

It transpired that Ivanova and Olga were part of a gang who were responsible for the murders of more than 40 people. Thirty of the gang were subsequently convicted, but another nine managed to evade arrest.

Female 'family' leaders

These and similar crimes perpetrated by felonious 'families' in the Old West and elsewhere may appear to be some of the random acts of violence and theft endemic in those brutal, lawless times, but they all have several significant elements in common. Each family was dominated by one personality, to whom all the other members were subservient. Invariably it was the mother, or an elder female, whose greed, disregard for life and contempt for the law corrupted and conditioned her brood to believe that they were entitled to take whatever belonged to others and if those individuals got in their way, then they deserved their fate. These were embittered and belligerent women who used their accomplices to punish those they resented and despised the most – hard-working, prosperous members of a society they felt had excluded them – by robbing them of their money, possessions and their lives. Such types 'personalize society', to use a phrase coined by the writer Colin Wilson, and seek revenge on it as a body rather than on the individuals they blame for their misfortune, but their primary target is invariably closer to home.

Carl Panzram

Wilson cites the case of American mass murderer Carl Panzram, who saw his crimes as revenge on a society that rejected him and his parents who sent him to the Minnesota State Training School, a correctional facility where he was raped and tortured. Panzram wrote: 'If I couldn't injure those who had injured me, then I would injure someone else.' Panzram suffered every punishment the US prison system meted out to him in stoic silence, while acknowledging that he had 'broken every law that had been made by man and God'. He professed to hate the entire human race and the brutality he experienced at the hands of the state penal system only compounded that belief. It seemed as if he invited punishment, to reinforce his belief that he was living in hell, a hell of his own making.

He was a martyr to the beatings that he knew his violent behaviour merited in that inhumane penal system of the 1920s, but a single act of kindness reduced him to tears. A guard gave him a dollar as a token gesture of sympathy after other guards had handed out a particularly severe beating, and that small gesture of fellow-feeling challenged the serial killer's lifelong belief that there was no compassion in a cruel world. It was the first step towards self-awareness and the questioning of his deeply ingrained misconceptions.

He then began writing his autobiography, *Killer, A Journal of Murder*, an account so shocking that it remained unpublished until 1970, 40 years after his death. It was a highly perceptive and eloquent

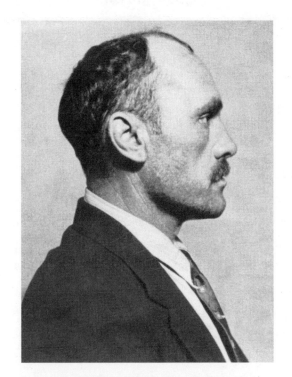

Carl Panzram murdered dozens in cold blood and met his end on the gallows.

confession, but it was too late to save its author from the gallows. He had murdered dozens in cold blood and had to pay the price.

'The Witch of Delray'

In 1931 48-year-old Rose Veres of Detroit, Michigan was arrested for the slaying of seven of her male tenants, whom she had killed for the insurance money. Her 18-year-old son, William, had been her willing accomplice and it was his incompetence which finally brought their murderous career to an end. He was seen helping his mother push a lodger to his death from an attic window. In addition, she was accused of the murder of three of her former husbands.

'The Witch of Delray', as she was dubbed by the press, was a Hungarian immigrant who protested that she could not speak English, although neighbours testified that she could. She attempted to hide behind her linguistic deficiency and her attorney argued that the accusations were nothing more than malicious neighbourhood gossip. He also claimed that it was customary for landladies in the Hungarian community to take out life insurance policies on behalf of their tenants.

Veres finally confessed to having murdered the last victim, 68-year-old Steven Mak, by pushing him from a window after she had put poison in his alcohol and his coffee.

'I tried to poison him twice, but he didn't die,' she admitted. 'So I pushed him out of the attic window. He was not dying fast enough.'

Leonarda Cianciulli

Ten years later, Italian mama Leonarda Cianciulli was convicted of murdering three middle-aged women and dismembering their bodies, which she boiled down to make soap, cakes and chocolate –

she gave the chocolate to local children. She managed to persuade the court that her adult son Giuseppe had taken no part in the killings, although it was subsequently proven that he had assisted her by throwing the women's bones into the river after she had first wrapped them in brown paper. It is believed that he also helped her to manhandle the bodies, which she could not have lifted alone. But at the time of her arrest she was desperate to prove that he had not helped her in dismembering the bodies and so she volunteered to take the judges to the city morgue, where she would dissect a corpse before their eyes in record time. They reluctantly agreed and were astonished when she carved up a corpse in less than 15 minutes. But they did not believe that she could have disposed of the bodies alone.

Leonarda had lured the women, who were all neighbours of hers, to her apartment in Correggio by promising to tell their fortunes. Had they been able to see into the future they would have refused her invitation, for Leonarda was obsessed with the idea of offering a blood sacrifice to some unspecified deity in order to save her son from having to enlist in the army. He was one of her four surviving children, eight having died in infancy. It is thought that the offering was made in the irrational belief that she would be lifting a curse placed on her surviving children by her own mother, who had given Leonarda 'the evil eye' on her death bed.

Drugged wine

The first to die was Faustina Setti, a lovelorn spinster who was told that her future husband was waiting for her in another town. She was persuaded to write letters to her friends and family informing them of the good news, but not to post them until she arrived. In this way Leonarda obtained the means of diverting suspicion from herself and creating a false trail.

Leonarda Cianciulli was the subject of a 1977 film, Gran Bollito, *or* Black Journal, *directed by Mauro Bolognini and starring Shelley Winters.*

On the day she was due to leave for her new life Faustina said her goodbyes to Leonarda and drank a toast to her future happiness, but the wine was drugged and Faustina was unable to defend herself against the blows of an axe wielded by her 'friend'. Her body was dismembered with a saw and a knife and the blood was collected for the rite.

In her published confession, Leonarda described the process with barely restrained glee.

> I threw the pieces into a pot, added seven kilos of caustic soda, which I had bought to make soap, and stirred the whole mixture until the pieces dissolved in a thick, dark mush that I poured into several buckets and emptied in a nearby septic tank. As for the blood in the basin, I waited until it had coagulated, dried it in the oven, ground it and mixed it with flour, sugar, chocolate, milk and eggs, as well as a bit of margarine, kneading all the ingredients together. I made lots of crunchy tea cakes and served them to the ladies who came to visit, though Giuseppe and I also ate them.

Leonarda used the same method to ensnare her second victim, Francesca Soavi, a widowed school teacher. This time she predicted that her victim would have a happy future as a governess in a school for young ladies in a distant town. Francesca was also duped into writing letters to her relatives and friends, which would lead them to believe that she had disappeared after moving to take up her duties. She was dispatched in the same brutal way and her blood offered to the unidentified deity.

The third to die was former La Scala opera singer Virginia Cacioppo, who was butchered on 30 September 1940.

'She ended up in the pot, like the other two,' confessed Leonarda, '. . . her flesh was fat and white. When it had melted I added a bottle of cologne, and after a long time on the boil I was able to make some most acceptable creamy soap. I gave bars to neighbours and acquaintances. The cakes, too, were better: that woman was really sweet.'

From each of her three victims Leonarda had obtained thousands of lire in cash in addition to jewellery and other valuables, so her claim to have killed the women just for their blood may not be the whole story.

Foolish errors

She might have continued to murder in this manner had not Cacioppo's sister-in-law raised the alarm after being told that Virginia had left suddenly for Florence, to work as a personal assistant to an unnamed impresario. It was unlike Virginia to have left without a word to her family, so the sister-in-law took her concerns to the police, informing them that she had last seen her sister-in-law entering the building where Leonarda lived. Leonarda may not have been a genuine fortune-teller, but she could read the signs when the police faced her with proof that she had cashed stolen bonds belonging to her third victim. She had also been foolish enough to give away stolen jewellery, which was identified as having belonged to Virginia Cacioppo.

At her trial in 1946, Leonarda made sure that the court knew about the sacrifice she had made for her country.

At her trial in Reggio Emilia last week Poetess Leonarda gripped the witness-stand rail with oddly delicate hands and calmly set the prosecutor right on certain details. Her deep-set dark eyes gleamed with a wild inner pride as she concluded: 'I gave the copper ladle, which I used to skim the fat off the kettles, to my country, which was so badly in need of metal during the last days of the war.'

Leonarda died in a criminal asylum in October 1970.

The grieving widow

In 1948 grieving widow Gertrude Brennan, aged 43, lured two love-hungry men to her Delaware farm using a 'lonely hearts' advertisement and then convinced her two grown sons, Raymond and Robert, to shoot them with a shotgun. They were the last of her victims to die before her arrest. Two years earlier she had persuaded her sons to drown an elderly woman, whose death had been falsely attributed to suicide. Mrs Brennan stubbornly resisted all attempts to make her confess, but after 26 hours of relentless questioning she finally broke down and admitted her crimes. The motive had been robbery. She had taken $1,500 (around $16,000/£12,500 today) from one victim and sold farm equipment and supplies belonging to the other to raise more cash.

A third potential victim, farmer Thomas Stretch of Canton, New Jersey, told police that he had visited the Brennans' farm shortly before their arrest and that they had treated him 'fine'. He too had answered the Black Widow's 'lonely hearts' advertisement, but believed that he had been allowed to walk away because he did not have any money on him that day.

'I looked over the farm and even stood by the pigpen [where the two bodies were buried],' he told a reporter. 'If I had any money I might have been alongside the men who are buried there.'

Gertrude's third son, George, then 17, admitted helping his mother and stepbrothers to bury the bodies, because he was frightened and

Grieving widow Gertrude Brennan used a 'lonely hearts' ad to lure love-hungry men to her Delaware farm.

felt he had to protect his mother, but he claimed that he had no idea what her motive had been.

'I can't understand why she killed those men. We were never in financial difficulty. All of us worked and turned over our money to her.'

Friends and relatives of the two missing men had reported their concerns to the police, who were able to trace the 'lonely hearts' letters to Mrs Brennan. After a brief trial Mrs Brennan and her son Robert were found guilty and given life sentences.

The McCrary-Taylor crime family

Other matriarchs saw crime as an alternative career choice, one which offered large rewards for very little effort and a minimal risk of arrest, provided that they coaxed their children and other family members into carrying out the robberies and slayings that they had planned.

Carolyn McCrary, a 45-year-old housewife from Santa Barbara, California was someone you wouldn't look at twice. With her thick-rimmed glasses, short red hair and unassuming features she could have passed for a supermarket cashier were it not for the fact that she was the brains behind a series of armed robberies and abductions, as well as 22 cold-blooded murders. All were committed with the willing participation of her 22-year-old daughter Ginger, her 19-year-old son Dennis, her son-in-law Raymond Taylor and her husband, Sherman.

The McCrary–Taylor gang were a crime family in the truest sense of the word. In the early 1970s, when Clint Eastwood was dealing out rough justice on the streets of 'Frisco as Dirty Harry on the big screen, Carolyn McCrary was offing people for real in the same state.

As a local newspaper reported at the time:

Theirs was a mean existence, which included an occasional brush with the law, nothing very serious, nothing that could be considered a harbinger of the future . . . For most of their lives, the men aimlessly wandered the American south-west, scratching for jobs as ranch hands, carnies and fry cooks.

The women worked honky-tonk carnivals too, or hustled jobs as waitresses in sad little cafes.

Finally, the family got fed up with the grubbiness of the toil and travail, but not of the nomadic life . . .

Its subsequent thrust for upward mobility resulted [. . .] in a cross-country crime spree, the extent of which may never be known.

At least 10 persons from Florida to Oregon were killed by one or another member of the family . . .

Short-lived success

Three of the victims were identified as donut shop waitresses, whose deaths netted the family no more than small change. But they were soon 'living well', according to police officers, after graduating to a spate of supermarket robberies which procured them a total of $46,000 ($270,000/£213,00 today). It got them out of their trailer homes and into two rented houses in an upper middle-class neighbourhood, the McCrary clan living in one property and the Taylors in the other.

They were also able to buy two station wagons, but were eventually traced through a vehicle they had used in one of the robberies, during which a police officer had been shot and badly wounded. Sherman had abandoned the car in his panic to escape. He and his son-in-law were initially convicted and sentenced for their part in the supermarket robbery and the other three members of the family were sentenced to nine months in jail for harbouring felons. But the investigation uncovered the family's participation in other offences and ballistics reports matched the weapons owned by the gang.

In all they were alleged to have murdered 22 people during 'high speed trips' across the country in an effort to escape. Sherman, Raymond and Dennis were convicted and received life sentences. Carolyn received a two-year sentence as an accessory after the fact and Ginger was granted immunity for implicating her father, mother and husband in the murder of Leeora Looney.

Children as crime accessories

Contrary to popular perception, serial killers are prevalent in every country. Even India has had its share of cruel, merciless murderers, most notorious of whom were the Gavit family of Maharashtra in western India.

In November 1996 mother Anjanabai, her adult daughters Seema and Renuka and Renuka's husband Kiran Shinde, were arrested and charged with the abduction of 13 babies and young children and the murder of nine. They had kidnapped some of the infants in the hope of forcing their parents to pay a ransom for their release, while the others were used to distract suspicion from the sisters, who had carried them while they moved among crowds stealing wallets and purses. As soon as the child grew too big or protested too loudly, it would be killed.

It was easy to snatch the infants from among distracted festival crowds, at bus stops, railway stations and outside temples – wherever people congregated and there was noise and confusion. But the family

Maharashtra in western India was the setting for an evil racket, where infants were kidnapped and ransoms were demanded for their release.

couldn't prevent their victims from crying for help or demanding to be returned to their homes. When three-year-old Pankaj complained to passers-by that he had been kidnapped, the Gavits mercilessly beat him to death.

Their last victim was killed as an act of pure vindictiveness against Anjanabai's estranged husband, who had abandoned his wife and two daughters. Shinde and Seema abducted his nine-year-old daughter, Kranti, whom their mother subsequently murdered. The sisters were arrested after the child's mother shared her suspicions with the police, who laid a trap for the girls when they attempted to abduct their father's other daughter.

Kiran Shinde was offered immunity in exchange for his testimony against his co-defendants and as a result of his statement the three women were convicted and sentenced to hang. Anjanabai died in prison in December 1997 aged 50, before her case could come to trial. Human rights lawyer and activist Asim Sarode told *The Hindu* newspaper:

> While I'm professionally and personally against the capital punishment, this is indeed one of the rarest of the rare cases where the perpetrators deserve the death sentence. The sisters' modus operandi was using small children, often toddlers, as diversions to distract the public while one of them was engaged in stealing purses. When in danger of being caught, the other used to throw or bang the child to the ground or any hard surface. The object was to elicit sympathy by manipulating the public's emotions. Their ordinariness makes their actions even more horrifying.

Death sentences upheld

It was alleged that after one of the children was thrown to the ground to distract attention from the sister who was engaged in picking pockets it was seriously injured and wouldn't stop crying. Anjanabai killed it by beating its head against a pole while her daughters continued eating their evening meal. Another child, 18-month-old Bhavna, was dismembered and the parts stuffed into a bag, which the sisters disposed of in the toilet of a local cinema. During the trial they admitted to having calmly sat through a film with the little body in the bag at their feet.

The death sentence aroused much public feeling and interest as the sisters would be the first women to be hanged in India in modern times, but in August 2006 the Supreme Court upheld the sentences, remarking:

> Going into the details of the case, we find no mitigating circumstances against them apart from the fact they are women. Further the nature of their crime and the systematic way in which each child was kidnapped and killed amply demonstrates the depravity of the mind of the appellants. They indulged in criminal activities for a very long period and continued till they were caught by the police. They very cleverly executed plans of kidnapping the children, and the moment they were no longer useful, killed them and threw the dead body at some deserted place.

Too smart for her own good

When you've been indicted on 118 separate charges ranging from forgery and fraud to murder, it's a sure bet you won't be at liberty for long. If Oklahoma-born serial killer Sante Kimes (born Sandra Louise Singhrs) had had any sense, she'd have pleaded guilty after her arrest in July 1998 and done her time, but being a lifelong con artist she convinced herself that she and her son Kenneth could fool the judge as they had fooled so many people before.

However, she was too clever for her own good and confessed to killings the pair hadn't committed in order to escape the death penalty. (In certain states a plea of guilty can result in a life sentence instead of execution.)

Sante was a wild child who is believed to have emigrated from the Dustbowl to Los Angeles during the Depression, where she grew up fleecing 'suckers' of their life savings. She was so addicted to enriching herself at the expense of others that she risked arrest on more than one occasion by burning down her own homes to claim the insurance money, rather than sell them for the same amount. And she also enslaved her maids rather than pay them, although she could easily have afforded to do so. Eventually she graduated to impersonating Hollywood celebrities such as actress Elizabeth Taylor, even if she bore little resemblance to the film star. It was while impersonating Taylor that she inveigled herself into a White House reception held by the then president, Gerald Ford.

Though she had come from humble beginnings, Sante liked to imagine that she was born for the high life. It seemed that she had achieved her dream when her ill-gotten fortune enabled her to move in high society, where she met and ensnared millionaire Kenneth Kimes. Kimes had made his fortune building a motel chain, but he lost it all defending a string of lawsuits brought by the couple's former 'employees', most of them homeless illegal immigrants who claimed they had been enslaved by Sante. They alleged that she had threatened to have them deported if they did not work for her without wages,

Sante Singhrs (right) with her future husband Kenneth Kimes meeting vice president Gerald Ford and his wife Betty in 1974.

allegations which saw her indicted on federal anti-slavery laws in August 1985 and sentenced to five years in prison.

Four years later she was released, but by this time she was carrying a chip on her shoulder the size of a house. It was then that the killings began.

Convicted by written accounts

The first victim was David Kazdin, who had been persuaded by Sante to use his name as a guarantor in a property deal and whose signature Sante subsequently forged in order to borrow $280,000 ($436,000/£345,000 today), with the house as security for the loan. Kazdin was killed by Kenneth Jnr in March 1998 in order to silence him, after he learned of the deception and threatened to go to the authorities. Together with an accomplice, mother and son disposed of the body in a waste dumpster near Los Angeles airport.

Having killed once, the next murder came more easily. Their second victim was 82-year-old millionaire Irene Silverman, who became suspicious after agreeing to rent her Manhattan mansion to the mother and son. Consequently, she too had to be silenced. In June 1998 Sante used a stun gun on the old woman and then her son strangled her. This time they dumped the body in a dumpster in Hoboken, New Jersey and Sante assumed the old woman's identity in order to continue living a life of luxury and hopefully gain access to the old lady's fortune.

Unbeknown to the killers, however, the old woman had made a written account of all that had taken place between her and her future murderers, while Kenneth Jnr had been foolish enough to detail the killing in his diary. Both accounts would be used to convict the mother and son of the murder during their trial, despite the fact that Irene Silverman's body had not been found. During the investigation Kenneth Jnr confessed to an earlier killing, that of banker Sayed Ahmed in the Bahamas in 1996. Kenneth boasted that they drowned him in the bathtub and then disposed of the body offshore.

Sante Kimes' lifelong career of fraud, deceit, theft and murder, together with her frequent irrational outbursts in court, led the judge to declare her a sociopath and a 'degenerate'. He then labelled her son Kenneth a 'remorseless predator' before handing down the maximum sentence to both of them.

During a second trial in June 2004, at which the pair faced charges of killing David Kazdin, Kenneth changed his plea to 'guilty' in order to save himself and his mother from the death penalty, although she continued to deny any part in the killing. Both were sentenced to life in prison, with Sante sent down for 120 years just to be certain that in her case life meant life.

'The Kebab Killer'

They called her 'The Kebab Killer' because Kabul housewife and mother Shirin Gul lured a series of men to their deaths with promises of sex, tea and kebabs (which were laced with powerful tranquillizers).

It is believed that she murdered at least 27 men with the help of her 18-year-old son, her lover, her first husband and his in-laws. Together they formed a murderous gang who made their fortune selling taxis belonging to the dead men, driving them across the border to Pakistan where they were sold with no questions asked. Shirin got her kicks spending her share of the proceeds on bling and shoes.

Among the 27 victims was her first husband, who had been killed by her lover after he was deemed surplus to her requirements. Eighteen of their victims were found buried in the back garden of her

Shirin Gul's lover Rahmat Ullah, who was accused of murdering 27 people along with Gul, and burying them in the yards of his various residences.

previous home in Jalalabad, which led to the discovery of half a dozen more at an address in Kabul.

Curiously, the killings of the taxi drivers had aroused little interest from the police, but they were forced into action after the body of a prominent businessman, Hanji Anwar, was discovered in June 2004. He had last been seen calling at Shirin's home under the pretext of negotiating a lucrative property deal.

Shirin received a 20-year sentence but allegedly continues to run a criminal empire from prison.

The piranha family

Inessa Tarverdiyeva and her second husband, Roman Podkopaev, were that rarest of aberrations, a serial killer couple who had managed to recruit the rest of their family into their homicidal activities. Odder still was the fact that the Russian pair had given their neighbours the impression that they were a respectable, suburban middle-class couple, while at the same time they were systematically planning the torture and murder of 30 innocent strangers for pleasure and profit.

Roman, a dentist and Inessa, a former nursery school teacher, styled themselves 'the Amazon Gang' and targeted affluent families, who were murdered for their electronic devices and other high-tech possessions. Six police officers died during the gang's criminal career, along with young children whom Inessa considered could be potential witnesses.

'I am a gangster by nature,' she boasted, adding that crime was a career choice that was no different from any other profession.

Until their arrest after a dramatic shoot-out in Aksai in the Rostov region in September 2013, the couple had embarked on a six-year crime spree aided and abetted by Roman's sister, Anastasia

Inessa Tarverdiyeva and her brother-in-law Sergei Sinelnik in the Rostov Region Court, 5 December 2017.

Sinelnik, and her husband, Sergei. He was a former policeman who was accused of having supplied the gang with information regarding the movements of fellow officers, who were subsequently ambushed and robbed. Inessa's teenage daughter (also called Anastasia) was a member of the gang at one time, as was her elder adopted sister Viktoria.

'The Amazon Gang' finally ran out of luck after Roman was stopped by the police following a failed robbery in which they killed the householders, only to discover that there was no cash in the house. When he was asked to produce his ID, Roman pulled a gun and killed one of the officers and wounded another. He rode off on a scooter with Viktoria but they were soon tracked down and a fierce gun battle ensued. Roman did not live to see the inside of a cell, having been shot dead while resisting arrest, but the rest of his family were overpowered and taken into custody. His widow attempted to lay the blame for the child killings on her dead husband, admitting only to shooting the adults.

During questioning, the women boasted of gouging out the eyes of two of their teenage victims and stabbing another 11-year-old girl 37 times, after shooting the girl's seven-year-old brother in the head. One of the two teenage girls was believed to have been Inessa's own god-daughter, who was tortured during a break-in at her home when the gang came to steal her father's hunting rifles.

As Joseph Conrad (1857–1924), the Polish-British novelist, wrote: 'The belief in a supernatural source of evil is not necessary; men alone are quite capable of every wickedness.'

Chapter Three:
Sadists and Sexual Predators

I think that if people are instructed about anything, it should be about the nature of cruelty. And about why people behave so cruelly to each other. And what kind of satisfactions they derive from it. And why there is always a cost, and a price to be paid.

Richard Russo (1949–), American novelist

Elizabeth and Mary Branch

Eighteenth-century England was a violent, lawless place where justice was dispensed swiftly with no possibility of appeal. Executions were as barbaric as the crimes themselves with public hangings drawing large, eager crowds. But even the most ardent opponent of capital punishment would have felt little compassion when Elizabeth and Mary Branch mounted the scaffold on 3 May 1740.

Sixty-seven-year-old Elizabeth and her 24-year-old daughter Mary had been convicted of the sadistic murder of their 13-year-old maid, Jane Buttersworth, and were suspected of murdering five more people, including Elizabeth's own mother and her husband, who had been poisoned after someone put arsenic in his food.

A contemporary account of the trial suggests that the case only came to light after the ghost of the murdered girl was seen hovering over her grave.

> It was obvious, judging by the suspicions of their neighbours, that both the accused had also committed other murders in the past. Mrs Branch's husband died under circumstances that led others who lived nearby to believe she had poisoned him and they were convinced that she had hanged her mother, after murdering her, to avoid an investigation into the cause of the death. Human bones were also discovered in a well near her farm, which were believed to be those of one of her servant girls who disappeared and was never heard from again.
>
> With such a reputation Mrs Branch found it difficult to get female staff in the locality and when she was in need of one she went further afield and brought Jane

| Beer, happy Produce of our Isle
Can sinewy Strength impart,
And wearied with Fatigue and Toil
Can chear each manly Heart. | Labour and Art upheld by Thee
Successfully advance,
We quaff Thy balmy Juice with Glee
And Water leave to France. | Genius of Health, thy grateful Taste
Rivals the Cup of Jove,
And warms each English generous Breast
With Liberty and Love. |

'Beer Street' by William Hogarth, a depiction of street life in the 18th century.

Buttersworth from Bristol. The young girl was hardly in the house before the two women subjected her to a brutal regime, and eventually beat her so savagely that she died. The older woman had Jane's corpse buried secretly in the graveyard and might have escaped blame, in spite of the complaint of her other maid, who had witnessed the murder and had been forced to lie next to her in bed, if a strange light had not been seen over the girl's grave, by several persons. This unearthly manifestation confirmed the neighbours' suspicions, and when the body was secretly removed at night, it was found by Mr Salmon, a surgeon, to be covered with wounds and other marks of violence.

The two women appear to have been compelled by the perverse pleasure they gained from inflicting pain on those who were in their power. As the daughter of a ship's surgeon, Elizabeth Parry had enjoyed a comfortable life and was lacking for little when she married gentleman farmer Benjamin Branch, for which she received a generous dowry of £2,000 (£380,000/$484,000 today) from her father.

After Branch died, the pair indulged in their sadistic games for ten years, which saw them graduate from torturing animals to abusing people. Former servants and neighbours testified to witnessing the beatings, which in Buttersworth's case were so severe that the flesh had been flayed down to the bone. Mother and daughter had beaten the girl almost continually for seven hours after they had accused her of taking too long to run an errand. Despite the testimony of eyewitnesses, Elizabeth thought she could evade justice and so took advantage of the lax and disorderly nature of the court at the Somerset assizes to bribe several jurors, which led to their dismissal.

'When sentence was passed the next day, the condemned elder woman complained bitterly to the court about the illegality of changing the jury, exclaiming that if she and her daughter had been tried by the first jury, they would not have been convicted.'

Gertrude Baniszewski

Evil is a term that is all too frequently and thoughtlessly applied to those whose behaviour is contrary to the norms of society, but sometimes there are no other words to express our revulsion and abhorrence of certain individuals' aberrant behaviour. Few would disagree that it was the only appropriate word to describe the sadistic acts committed by Indiana housewife and mother Mrs Gertrude Baniszewski, who tortured her teenage foster child Sylvia Likens to death in 1965. Sylvia and her younger sister Jenny were boarded with Mrs Baniszewski after their parents separated. The girl's father, an itinerant carnival worker, paid her $20 ($162/£128 today)a week to 'straighten his girls out' and later admitted that he had not taken the trouble to investigate the kind of people he was entrusting his daughters to.

Mrs Baniszewski's cruelty began with beatings and cigarette burns to Sylvia's skin, public humiliation in front of the neighbourhood children and sexual abuse involving the insertion of objects into her private parts. Her demented foster parent imagined it would help 'cure' Sylvia of her natural desires.

Sylvia was imprisoned in the cellar, denied the use of the bathroom and subjected to scalding baths to cure her of her 'sins'. On top of that, her stomach was scored with a hot needle spelling out the word 'prostitute'.

During this prolonged systematic physical abuse, Mrs Baniszewski enlisted the help of her own children and even some boys from the neighbourhood. When Sylvia died, the pathologist identified 150 wounds on her body.

At the trial of the five defendants – mother-of-seven Mrs Baniszewski, her daughter Paula, her son John aged 13 and two neighbourhood boys – 20 witnesses testified to the fortnight of abuse which ended in Sylvia's death from a brain haemorrhage, shock and malnutrition on 26 October 1966.

At the end of the five-week trial Mrs Baniszewski was found guilty of first-degree murder and sentenced to life imprisonment, her daughter was convicted of second-degree murder and John and the two 15-year-old neighbourhood youths were found guilty of the lesser crime of manslaughter. As so often happens in such cases, there were emotional scenes at the trial. There was much hand-wringing and copious tears were shed by the accused – not for their victims but for themselves. Mrs Baniszewski expressed no remorse, only sickening self-pity, but she made a pathetically melodramatic plea for clemency on the grounds that she had been 'depressed' at the time and had been under the influence of medication. The two youths who were convicted of manslaughter for their part in the torture and death of Sylvia Likens wept openly, but again they were grieving for themselves.

Lyudmila and Sasha Spesivtsev

The former Soviet Union refused to acknowledge the existence of serial killers. In fact, the only 'criminals' Stalin and his successors acknowledged were political dissidents and other enemies of the state. But since the fall of the communist empire Russia has been forced to admit to having its share of deviants.

Top of the list must surely be Siberian school employee Lyudmila Spesivtsev, who enticed teenage girls to her home so that her son

'Sasha' (Alexander) could rape, torture and cannibalize them. His mother then served up the choicest cuts for her depraved offspring to devour.

The pair had repeatedly refused anyone access to their apartment, which should have aroused suspicions. Had anyone been allowed inside they would have found the walls splattered with blood and the rooms reeking of rotting human remains. The victims were dismembered in the bath, often with the help of 'Sasha's' current sex slave, who feared she would share the same fate if she didn't do as she was told. As a result, the kitchen and bathroom resembled an abattoir.

One can only wonder why the neighbours did not report the stifled screams of the victims and the sounds of their struggles. They certainly complained of the putrid stench coming from the apartment on many occasions and protested about the incessant loud music which Sasha turned up in an attempt to cover the cries of his victims.

When the police entered the apartment, they found a headless corpse in the bath and a severely mutilated girl in the throes of death. She survived just long enough to give them an account of her ordeal, which sealed the fate of her tormentors, who had no hope of talking their way out of a death sentence.

Body parts in river

'Sasha' was not unknown to the authorities. He had been convicted of murdering a girlfriend, but had been sent to an asylum for the criminally insane and was only released when the doctors were convinced he was no longer a threat to society.

When he was not torturing girls, he spent his time brooding on the imagined ills of society and writing demented theses attacking democracy. He identified its most vulnerable victims as being the homeless street urchins who begged for bread and spare change on the streets of his home town, Novokuznetsk. After he approached them with a promise of food or work they were never seen alive again.

But 'Sasha' was either too arrogant or too crazy to think much about the problem of disposing of the remains. He simply threw them into the local river and hoped they would be washed away. Inevitably, though, some of the body parts were washed up on the bank and this aroused the interest of the police.

Mother and son were finally arrested in October 1996 and both were found guilty of 19 murders (the couple were suspected of many more killings, but a number of victims remained unidentified due to lack of public funds for forensic tests). Sasha recorded the grisly details of 80 murders in his diary, but police suspected that some of these could have been no more than his sick fantasies.

Lyudmila remained stubbornly mute throughout her trial and escaped with a 13-year prison sentence, but she was not permitted to live in peace as a vigilante group formed on a social networking site, calling for her to be lynched. She had been an active and willing accomplice to her son's crimes, having induced his last female victims to visit their flat by promising them money if they helped her move some furniture. Once inside, the two terrified 13-year-old girls were confronted by her homicidal son and his ferocious Doberman. Twenty-six-year-old 'Sasha' was spared execution on the grounds of insanity and was returned to the asylum.

Eva Cummings and Luke Wright

New York homicide cops have investigated every depraved act on the statute books, but even they were shocked by the depths to which 51-year-old Eva Cummings had fallen when they charged her with coercing her 31-year-old mentally retarded son Luke Wright into repeatedly raping, torturing and abusing his 23-year-old severely mentally disabled half-sister, Laura. She had been hooded and tied to a chair for the last eight weeks of her life before her mother suffocated her in January 2010.

During a week-long trial a prosecution lawyer remarked that the best day of Laura's life was the day she died. The police admitted that the case was one of the most sickening they had ever investigated and were convinced that Luke had been manipulated by a 'wicked, evil' mother, who received a 52 years-to-life sentence for the second-degree murder of her daughter. Luke, who has an IQ of 52, was sentenced to 40 years in jail.

Luke's two brothers, Edward and Richard, testified against him, but laid the blame on their mother, claiming that she was a control freak who frequently refused to give them even a couple of dollars for a candy bar and forbade them from seeing their friends.

Luke's lawyer had argued that his client's mental deficiencies – incurred during severe childhood beatings with bricks and baseball bats – meant that he could not be held accountable for his actions, but the prosecution convinced the jury that his detailed confessions and other admissions revealed that he knew what he was doing was wrong.

Neighbours did not intervene

It would be nothing more than yet another distressing case in the files of the New York Police Department were it not for the questions it raised regarding the culpability of the social services and the lack of intervention or even interest exhibited by Luke and Eva's neighbours. Journalist Matt Chandler of bizjournals.com was one of those who asked questions.

While much of the Wright case focused on the nature of the crimes and the 'house of horrors' that he, his half-sister and mother, Eva Cummings, lived in, there is another issue that has been at times overlooked: Why didn't anyone step forward to save the life of a mentally disabled young woman who was unable to fight for herself?

Chandler highlighted the fact that North Collins, the scene of the crime, was a small and friendly community whose residents might be expected to take a discreet interest in their neighbours.

The escalating abuse over the years was at times reported to authorities, but for the most part, it appears people simply looked the other way while a disabled girl was slowly and methodically used, abused, tortured and eventually murdered. What does this say about our society? Have we fallen this far as to act with utter indifference toward another human being just because they may not be related to us?

How often do we see cases of people acting with indifference because they 'don't want to get involved'.

Chandler cited countless incidents where seemingly callous bystanders chose to ignore an injured or ailing person in the street and continued their mobile phone conversations or carried on munching on their burger because they didn't want to appear to care for the welfare of a stranger. It is possible that their apparent indifference may hide the fact that they were worried that they would be 'suckered' into giving money to someone who was faking a heart attack or that they would be held liable if there was litigation resulting from an assault or an accident.

As Chandler observed: 'What happened in North Collins shouldn't come as any great surprise . . . their inaction says a lot about what is so wrong in our society today. And it is a sad commentary on the value (or better yet, lack of value) we put on another person's life.'

Killing for family 'honour'

> There is no value of life without honour.
>
> *Mohammad Shafia*

On the morning of Tuesday 30 June 2009 the bodies of four Asian females were recovered from the Rideau canal at Kingston Mills Locks, in Canada. Fifty-two-year-old Rona Amir Mohammad and her three 'nieces', the Shafia sisters – 19-year-old Zainab, 17-year-old Sahar and 13-year-old Geeti – had apparently drowned after their Nissan Sentra plunged into the deep water and sank too rapidly to give them time to swim to safety. Curiously, none of the dead occupants had been wearing seat belts and the rear right passenger window was wound down. Had they been alive when the vehicle sank, at least one of them would have been able to escape and swim to the surface and call for help.

The autopsies would reveal that three of the victims had bruises to the backs of their heads, suggesting that they had been hit before they had been forcibly held under water. It was only then, when they were either dead or unconscious, that they were manhandled back into the vehicle, which was then shunted off the road into the canal.

As soon as Detective Constable Geoff Dempster began to sift through the evidence, something else made him suspicious. All

The bodies of four Asian females were recovered from Kingston Mills Locks, Kingston, Ontario in 2009.

four women evidently took a pride in their appearance and were fashionably dressed. Sahar had had her belly button pierced and her nails were painted two different colours (purple on her fingers and black on her toes), Geeti had a navel ring and their 'aunt' Rona (their father's first wife) wore three pairs of earrings and six gold bangles. And yet Zainab had gone to her death with her cardigan on backwards.

Shortly after DC Dempster was summoned to police headquarters the dead girls' father, Mohammad Shafia, their mother Tooba and their 18-year-old brother Hamed arrived to file a missing person's report. They were interviewed separately, and their testimony was videotaped.

They each stuck to the same story. The family, recent immigrants to Canada, had been on a road trip from their home in Montreal to Niagara Falls and were staying overnight at a motel in Kingston, Ontario when Zainab borrowed the car keys to retrieve some clothes. The next morning the Nissan and the four women were nowhere to be found. Their parents said they assumed that they had decided to go for a midnight drive, but had missed a turning and gone off the road into the canal.

Betrayed no emotion

DC Dempster was a highly experienced officer and he had seen many grieving relatives, but Mohammad, Tooba and Hamed did not appear to be in shock. Instead, they were unnaturally calm. Not one of the three betrayed any emotion and Dempster could not believe it was due to their way of dealing with death. Whatever the culture, surely one of them would have cracked at some point and grieved for their loved ones.

And Dempster was troubled by their inability or unwillingness to answer the questions that bothered him more as the day wore on. Why had the women gone for a night-time drive after travelling for six hours that day? Even if one or more of them couldn't sleep and the motel had nothing to offer after midnight, it seemed like an odd thing to do. Moreover, why did the parents and brother arrive at the police station in a minivan and not in the Lexus they had been driving the previous day?

Hamed told his interrogator that he had been unable to sleep and had driven the Lexus all the way back to Montreal to collect the laptop he had left at home. As soon as his father phoned to tell his son that the girls were missing, Hamed claimed to have driven the 300 km (186 miles) back to the motel in a Pontiac minivan because it used less fuel than the Lexus. It struck the detective that this was an odd thing to consider in the early hours of the morning after the boy had been informed that his aunt and sisters had disappeared. His suspicions and the witness testimony were sufficient to obtain a warrant to tap the Shafias' phone and in one damning call the police heard the confession they could not prise out of the parents in the days and weeks that followed the tragedy.

'They haven't done good,' Mohammad was heard to say, 'and God has punished them . . . They betrayed kindness, they betrayed Islam, they betrayed our religion and creed, they betrayed our tradition, they betrayed everything.'

Culture clash

But it wasn't God who had punished the girls for the perceived 'dishonour' they had brought to the family. It was their parents, specifically their fanatically religious father, who had been behind the wheel of the Lexus that night and had shunted the Nissan into the canal and watched with grim satisfaction as the four women went to their deaths. If anyone 'betrayed' the family honour it was Mohammad, by this one cruel act of infanticide spawned from religious fanaticism.

As Michael Friscolanti wrote for MacLeans on 3 March, 2016:

Before they died, the Shafia sisters were caught in the ultimate culture clash, living in Canada but not allowed to be Canadian. They were expected to behave like good Muslim daughters, to wear the hijab and marry a fellow Afghan. And when they rebelled against their father's 'traditions' and 'customs'—covertly at first, then for all the community to see—the shame became too much to bear. Only a mass execution (staged to look like a foolish wrong turn) could wash away the stain of their secret boyfriends and revealing clothes . . . His daughters died because they were defiant and beautiful and had dreams of their own. Because they were considered property, not people. But the two words at the heart of this sensational case—'honour killing'—do not tell the whole twisted tale.

Second bride

Mohammad Shafia was a self-educated and self-made man. An entrepreneur from a middle-class Afghan family, he built a successful international import-export business specializing in electronics, through astute deals and hard bargaining. When it came to his family life, he was equally uncompromising.

His first marriage to Rona Amir, the daughter of a retired military officer, in February 1979, was an arranged marriage that failed to provide the heir he wanted. He took his disappointment and frustration out on his wife, belittling and bullying her until she consented to his taking another bride. Her successor was 17-year-old Tooba, who was then half Mohammad's age and whose presence in the family home was a constant reminder to Rona of her 'failure' to fulfil her marital obligations and duty, as her husband saw it. Rona kept a secret diary in which she described the first ten years of her marriage as 'torture' and the arrival of Tooba as 'a new catastrophe'.

The two women were forced to live in an uneasy harmony, which became severely strained when Tooba gave birth to a daughter, Zainab, in September 1989 and subsequently a son, Hamed. In her diary Rona described Tooba as constantly scheming to separate her from her estranged husband. After the birth of a second daughter, Sahar, in October 1991, Mohammad stopped sleeping with Rona and she had to content herself with raising the child as her own, having been given Sahar as 'compensation' by her younger rival.

Move to Canada

The birth of two more children, who could not be named in the press for legal reasons, put further strain on the polygamous marriage as their parents connived to turn them against their older siblings. These children grew up to distrust and despise their sisters and were so conditioned to see them as 'betraying' the family that they defended their mother and father in court, even after the undeniable evidence of their parents' guilt had been put before them.

In June 2007 the family, now comprising three adults and seven children, emigrated to Canada without Rona. She was sent to live with relatives in Europe while Mohammad tried to think of a way of bringing her over, as he needed her to look after the children. She was excluded from the family migration due to Canada's immigration laws, which allowed for only one spouse.

Mohammad's first act on arriving in Quebec was to buy a silver Lexus, acquire a $2 million (£1.6m) strip mall and build a $900,000 (£712,000) mansion in an exclusive suburb of Montreal. Six months later, Rona entered the country using a temporary visa issued to her on the understanding that she was his 'cousin' and was to be employed as his children's unpaid nanny.

While Mohammad was away on business Tooba and Hamed were, according to one source, 'his eyes, his ears and his fists'. Tooba reportedly greeted Rona on her arrival by reminding the older woman: 'Your life is in my hands. You are my servant.' And Hamed kept his 18-year-old sister Zainab a virtual prisoner in her room for ten months after she had invited a Pakistani classmate home for an innocent visit. Zainab was prevented from returning to school and her male friend was 'discouraged' from seeing her again.

Suicide bid

Sixteen-year-old Sahar attempted suicide by mixing silica gel from a shoebox with water after Tooba had created a scene at the school in front of her classmates when she heard that she had been seen kissing a boy. Sahar was violently sick but didn't die, thanks to the timely intervention of Geeti and Rona, but Tooba refused to help her and told her stepmother and sister that the girl could 'go to hell' for all she cared.

As a punishment for kissing the boy – not for attempting to take her own life – Tooba ordered the family to exclude her and not speak to her under any circumstances. Under intolerable pressure and by now severely depressed, Sahar sought help from the school. They in turn called in the child welfare services on 7 May 2008 and it was this flagrant act of defiance, as her parents saw it, which condemned Sahar, together with her sisters and 'aunt' Rona, to an early death.

By the time the social worker arrived at the school, the teenager had withdrawn her request for help. Clearly intimidated by her parents and fearing what reprisals they might take if an outsider was called in to investigate her home life, she recanted. When her parents arrived even Zainab, her fellow sufferer, was too scared to confirm the accusations. Their father's hostility and his threat to sue the school and the welfare services brought the matter to an abrupt and unsatisfactory end. The sisters went home and suffered a further year of abuse, both verbal and physical, until Zainab sought refuge at a women's shelter, ten weeks before she died. Her furious father saw it as a gross act of disloyalty and decided to punish her.

The more he brooded on her 'betrayal', the more he persuaded himself that his daughter had been encouraged in her rebellion by her wilful sisters and his first wife, Rona, whom he considered a liability. If the authorities discovered their true relationship the whole family would be deported for entering the country under false pretences.

Rona happened to overhear a conversation between Mohammad, Tooba and Hamed in which Mohammad informed his wife and son that he intended to murder Zainab and 'the other one' while he was at it. She assumed 'the other one' was a reference to her and was so terrified that she phoned her sister in France, who told her not to worry, that such things do not happen in Canada.

Murder research

For all Mohammad's claims to be protecting the 'honour' of his family and his religion, he was not devout. He had not prayed at a mosque since arriving in Canada and so when Zainab returned home on condition that she would be allowed to marry her Pakistani boyfriend, her stepmother had to ask an uncle to organize the ceremony. Within 24 hours Zainab was married and divorced after caving in to Tooba's hysterical reaction, during which she affected a fainting fit. Zainab then offered to sacrifice her happiness and her husband's if she would stop crying.

But she was still in a hysterical state when the uncle phoned Mohammad to tell him the 'good news'. Mohammad was abroad on business and was not placated by the uncle's offer to marry Zainab to one of his sons to remove the 'stain' from her reputation.

'If I was there, I would have killed her,' Mohammad told him.

Mohammad's resolve to murder her sister hardened when Hamed flew out to join him and showed him pictures he had taken of Sahar and her boyfriend. Two days later, on 3 June, the first of a series of incriminating Google searches were made on Hamed's laptop. Someone wanted to know if convicted prisoners would lose control of their property while they were in prison. Further searches were made into the location of lakes in Quebec.

On their return, they learned that 13-year-old Geeti was being disruptive at school and had been caught shoplifting. Evidently, her unhappy home life was affecting her behaviour and prompting her to act in a way that would draw attention to her. It was a cry for help that went unnoticed by the school but not by her father. In his mind, she could not be relied upon to keep quiet when Zainab, Sahar and Rona were silenced, so she would have to perish with them.

Hamed was now engaged in serious research into the subject of murder online and was driving hundreds of kilometres from their home to find the perfect location in which to stage the 'accident'. Although the murders were motivated by irrational fears for family 'honour' and charged by emotion, they were clinically planned.

Trial and imprisonment

Ignorance, the root and stem of all evil.

Socrates (470–399 BC)

After a trial lasting six weeks Mohammad, Tooba and Hamed were all convicted of quadruple murder in the first degree – premeditated murder – and sentenced to life in prison. They would not be eligible for parole for 25 years.

In summing up, Justice Maranger told the accused:

> It is difficult to conceive of a more heinous, more despicable, more honourless crime. The apparent reason behind these cold-blooded, shameful murders was that the four completely innocent victims offended your twisted notion of honour – a notion of honour that is founded on the domination and control of women, a sick notion of honour that has absolutely no place in any civilized society.

When the police wiretapped their house during the investigation, Tooba was heard to bemoan her fate and blame God for visiting such tragedy upon them.

She could not accept that her fate and that of her husband and son was entirely of their own making.

Mexican death cult

What attracts some people to worship the Divine and others the Devil is one of the enduring mysteries of human nature and one which has puzzled theologians and criminal psychologists alike. It appears that some aberrant personalities are driven by an irresistible compulsion to provoke outrage as a means of attracting attention to themselves. They consider themselves above what they see as the petty constraints of civilized society and deliberately flout its morality, acting conversely to its laws in order to set themselves apart from those they despise. In doing so they delude themselves into believing that they are superior.

A reveller dressed as La Santa Muerte or our Lady of the Holy Dead.

Others cynically masquerade as Devil worshippers to justify their brutality and the exploitation of their credulous followers.

Silvia Meraz Moreno and her son Ramon Palacios were the leaders of a violent cult in Nacozari, Mexico which worshipped La Santa Muerte, the female Saint of Death. After their arrest in March 2012, the Morenos claimed that their deity demanded human sacrifice and so they persuaded eight adult members of their extended family to collaborate in the abduction and murder of three strangers – two ten-year-old boys and a middle-aged male – who were then sacrificed on the altar to La Santa Muerte. Their throats and wrists were slit and their blood was collected in a vessel to be poured upon the altar.

Silvia told her interrogators that she sincerely believed that her black goddess would reward her with money, but the authorities suspected that the killings were related to the family's involvement in narcotics. Blood sacrifice is practised by several notorious Mexican drug cartels.

Shrinking family

More bewildering are the cases involving two or more members of one family who conspire to murder their own, particularly when they do not attempt to justify the crime by claiming self-defence or abuse.

Missouri mother Diane Staudte and her 22-year-old daughter Rachel confessed in June 2013 to the murder of two family members and the attempted murder of a third, just because these individuals got on their nerves. Diane confessed to hating her husband, Mark, her 26-year-old son, Shaun and her eldest daughter Sarah, all of whom she poisoned with drinks laced with antifreeze. Sarah miraculously survived.

Mexican graveyard: Silvia Meraz Moreno told her followers that their deity demanded human sacrifice.

Chapter Four:
Killer Couples

Idle people are often bored and bored people, unless they sleep a lot, are cruel. It is no accident that boredom and cruelty are great preoccupations in our time.

Renata Adler (1937–), American author

Deadly duos

Serial killer couples are rare, but psychological assessments of those who have been convicted reveal that they share several traits and

'A boy's best friend is his mother' – Anthony Perkins on the set of Psycho. In the twisted mind of a psychopath, the maternal relationship can take on a whole new meaning.

factors in their upbringing. They have invariably suffered severe abuse in childhood and have witnessed abnormal sexual practices, which has distorted their perception of what constitutes a healthy human relationship.

Rosemary and Fred West were raised to believe that incest and other deviant behaviour was perfectly normal. Consequently, their toxic upbringing led them to become emotionally dependent on each other and to isolate themselves from what they imagined to be a hostile world that would not accept them or understand such behaviour. They needed each other to reinforce their distorted view of the world and the potential threat they imagined was posed by outsiders.

In such relationships, the women tend to be much younger than their male partners and to have had no criminal record at the time of their first meeting, while the men are likely to have committed serious crimes. This aura of criminality appears to attract the type of female who is seeking illicit excitement and it strengthens their devotion.

Sarah and Gordon Northcott

As Norman Bates observed in Alfred Hitchcock's slasher primer *Psycho*: 'A boy's best friend is his mother.' But in the twisted mind of the psychopath that relationship can take on another meaning entirely. In the case of Sarah Jane Northcott and her son Gordon, a mother's instinct to protect her 'boy' crossed over the line into complicity in a series of horrific murders which shocked 'jazz age' America.

In the 1920s, serial killers and sexual predators were thought to be a rare phenomenon and the general public could be said to have had a rather simplistic notion of what they might look like and how they behaved, thanks to the image created by lurid 'penny dreadfuls', racy dime novels and silent movie serials. So when a Los Angeles

Gordon Northcott and his mother Sarah Jane who also claimed to be his grandmother, which must have been confusing.

mother and her adult son were accused of abducting and butchering children, many refused to believe the sensational headlines. Even the local police suspected that the boys had simply run away from home and would eventually turn up unharmed.

The first indication that a major murder case was about to be uncovered came in September 1928 when a distraught Canadian mother, Winnefred Clark, reported that her 15-year-old son, Sanford, was being sexually abused by his own uncle. Sanford had been sent to live with Gordon Stewart Northcott and his mother Sarah two years earlier, but a series of letters, supposedly written by the boy, made Winnefred suspicious, so she sent her daughter Jessie to Los Angeles to investigate. Jessie returned in a highly distressed state. Not only was the boy being abused, but she herself had only narrowly escaped being raped by her 'Uncle' Gordon. When the police arrived at the Northcott farm, both mother and son had disappeared, leaving nephew Sanford alone and terrified.

Bodies in shallow graves

Sanford told the police that he had been forced to participate in the kidnapping of other boys and had witnessed their rape and murder. He led them to two shallow graves and the murder weapons – two axes still matted with blood and hair. The bodies could not be readily identified due to decomposition and the primitive nature of forensic pathology at the time, but several personal items, including Boy Scout badges and handwritten letters, were found at the scene and were subsequently identified as belonging to the missing boys.

However, there was no trace of nine-year-old Walter Collins, who had disappeared on 10 March. Witnesses had reported seeing what they took to be a child's body wrapped in newspaper on the back seat of a car on that day, but it had driven off before they could confront the 'foreign-looking' driver and his passenger.

The Northcotts had fled across the border into Canada, but they were soon apprehended and brought back to the United States for trial. Gordon Northcott confessed to five murders, including that of Walter Collins, whose body had indeed been in the back of the car, but he hinted that he might have killed as many as 20 young men. He was convicted and executed.

His mother admitted to being an accomplice and told the court that they had both used an axe on each victim so that they would share responsibility. She attempted to explain her son's behaviour by claiming that her husband had raped their own daughter, Winnefred, and that she was Gordon's real mother, but the jury regarded this as yet another lie and found her guilty of abduction and murder, for which she received a life sentence. Her grandson, Sanford, was questioned further and judged to be not entirely without blame, whether he had been forced into helping the Northcotts, as he claimed, or not. He was sent to a young offenders' institution.

The bad seeds – Gerald and Charlene Gallego

'Bad seed' California killer Gerald Gallego claimed he was destined to be a criminal because he had been 'infected' with 'bad blood'. On his arrest in November 1980, the 34-year-old told detectives investigating a series of brutal murders that both of his parents had been career criminals and therefore he was genetically predisposed to a life of crime.

His father had been executed for killing two policemen and his mother was a prostitute whose clients would abuse the boy. It was said that he had begged for affection, but she neglected him and beat him whenever she was drunk or high on drugs. He later boasted that he had been burglarizing neighbouring houses from the age of six and that it was a matter of record that he had been sent to a young offenders' institution at the age of 12 for committing indecent acts with a six-year-old girl. But he had not been rehabilitated. Three years later he was inside again, after being convicted of armed robbery.

On his release, he seduced and married a series of women, all of whom suffered beatings and abuse from a man one of them called a real-life 'Jekyll and Hyde'. As soon as he had spent their money, he grew tired of them and became even more abusive until they were forced to divorce him.

By December 1980 the case against Gallego and his latest wife Charlene, his alleged partner in nine brutal sex murders, was in danger of collapsing because Sacramento County couldn't finance a prosecution. Outraged residents took up collections to raise the money to ensure the couple were convicted and stayed behind bars. In total they raised $28,000 ($80,000/£63,000 today), enough to hire a prosecution team to challenge Gallego's attorney, who argued that his client had post-traumatic stress disorder as a result of the extreme abuse he had suffered as a child and head injuries that had left him brain-damaged. As a consequence, he was supposedly 'incapable of planning, problem-solving, comprehending or making judgements'.

Willing assistant

Incredibly, Gallego had no trouble persuading his soon-to-be seventh wife, two-time divorcee Charlene Williams, that he had a right to abuse her when she roused his anger for any reason, or failed to satisfy his insatiable sexual appetite. But then she too was a deeply disturbed personality and seemed to consent to everything he did, including,

Charlene and Gerald Gallego in court in Sacramento.

allegedly, sodomizing his own teenage daughter, whom he had been abusing since she was six.

California-born Charlene was just 24 at the time she was questioned about her role in 11 killings, though the couple were eventually charged with only three murders. She was said to have been an intelligent, well-spoken child who had travelled with her father, the vice president of a supermarket chain, and helped him with his business. But in her teens she took to using drugs and boasting of fantasy lovers. Her previous relationships appear to have failed because of her aggressive sexuality, which led her to demand that her male lovers agree to a threesome with another woman. When her married lovers refused, Charlene attempted suicide.

She was seriously troubled by the time she met her match in Gerald Gallego, a man who freely admitted liking rough sex, and they soon became inseparable. Gallego was the dominant partner and Charlene was submissive. Had they not dragged anyone else into their bizarre and violent relationship, they might have found a freakish kind of contentment together, but Gerald was also a sexual predator who became turned on at the thought of raping unwilling victims.

Charlene, too, liked the idea of having sex with young girls and exercising control over helpless victims with her lover, but she only became fully committed to his evil activities in the summer of 1978, when she agreed to assist him in abducting young girls to rape and torture. That September the couple cruised the streets of Sacramento in their Dodge van looking for potential victims. On 11 September, they abducted 17-year-old Rhonda Scheffler and 16-year-old Kippi Vaught from a shopping centre by offering them a joint. Once inside the van the girls were threatened with a gun and told that Gallego would shoot them if they screamed. They were then bound and gagged before being driven to a remote location outside town, where Gallego repeatedly raped them while Charlene watched. After that, they drove the girls to a secluded site, where they were beaten with a tyre lever and then shot. Their bodies were then dumped by the roadside.

Irresistible bloodlust

A fortnight later Charlene and Gerald were married. They celebrated the event in Houston, Texas, where they signed the hotel register using false names. Gallego's daughter had filed charges against her father alleging incest and unlawful intercourse, which meant that he was now a fugitive, but that didn't dampen his unnatural cravings, which overcame any fear that he might be caught.

On 24 June 1979 the couple drove to a county fair, confident of finding more young girls to abuse. Two unsuspecting victims, 14-year-old Brenda Lynne Judd and 13-year-old Sandra Kaye Colley, were enticed into the van with the promise of payment for distributing leaflets. Neither had suspected that Charlene was procuring for a serial rapist and sadistic killer. After Gerald had satisfied his lust, he smashed their skulls in with a hammer and dumped their bodies in the Nevada desert. There was no reason to fear that the bodies would ever be found. And if they were, wild animals and the weather would have long erased any forensic traces of their killers.

For nearly a year after that Gerald appeared to have kept his bloodlust under control, or at least to have satisfied it in other ways. He found a job as a bartender back home in Sacramento, using his alias, but on 24 April 1980 he was overcome with a need to repeat the horrific killings of two young girls yet again, as if it was a sickening ritual rather than a random act of lust and violence.

This time the victims were two 17-year-olds, Karen Chipman Twiggs and Stacy Ann Redican, whom Charlene again lured into the van with the promise of a joint. Both were beaten to death with a hammer after Gerald had satisfied his perverted sexual desires and were buried in shallow graves near Lovelock, Texas.

That June the couple abducted 21-year-old Linda Aguilar, as she thumbed a lift on the highway. She too made the fatal mistake of assuming that she would come to no harm by hitching with a married couple, but she was also raped and beaten senseless, before being buried alive. She was four months pregnant at the time.

Died before his execution

On 17 July 1980 Gerald celebrated his 34th birthday by kidnapping barmaid Virginia Mochel, whom he raped and strangled with a nylon fishing line. The unfeeling couple dumped her body in undergrowth near Clarksburg.

By this time Gerald believed himself to be invincible. He thought he could operate alone, without Charlene, and on 2 November he forced 22-year-old Craig Miller and 21-year-old Mary Sowers into the van at gunpoint in broad daylight and in full view of their friends. None of them, however, had seen the gun. They thought it odd that Craig and Mary had left without explanation and with a man they had never seen before, but fortunately one of the friends had the presence of mind to make a note of the registration number and when Craig and Mary failed to return, they called the police.

But before the police could trace the van, their friends were dead. Gerald had killed Craig then taken Mary to his own apartment, where he raped her while Charlene, who was pregnant at the time, watched impassively. Then the Gallegos drove their latest victim to a remote location, where Gerald shot her. This time he made sure his victim was dead. He fired three bullets into her and then walked away.

However, on this occasion the police arrived before the couple had time to clean the van. They found spent bullet casings, reels of duct tape and other incriminating evidence, which forced Charlene to confess in exchange for a promise that she would not face charges in another state, one which authorized the death penalty.

She was subsequently convicted and sentenced to 16 years and eight months in prison, but remained unrepentant, telling her interrogators: 'We had this sexual fantasy, see, so we just carried it out . . . I mean, like, it was easy and fun and we really enjoyed it. So why shouldn't we do it?'

Gerald was sentenced to death in June 1983 for the killings of Mary Sowers and Craig Miller. At a separate trial the following year he received a second death sentence for the killings of Karen Twiggs and Stacy Redican. But the appeals process was prolonged, because Gerald was desperate to drag it out and savour the spotlight for as long as he could.

In March 1999 Gerald instructed his lawyers to appeal against the remaining death sentence on the grounds of insanity and affected all the symptoms he could think up in support of his claim. He died of cancer on 18 July 2002, while appealing his sentence.

The 'Ken and Barbie Killers'

The wedding photos capture a happy couple seated in the back of a hired limousine: the handsome groom flashing a brilliant white smile, elegant in his blue satin suit, his 21-year-old bride beaming at the camera in a fairy tale wedding dress, a large bunch of white roses on her lap. They were every photographer's ideal of the perfect young couple, but only a fortnight before they had abducted, raped, murdered and dismembered a 14-year-old girl just for kicks.

Paul and Karla Bernardo were habitual sexual predators soon to be convicted of a series of horrific torture-murders, including the rape

Karla Homolka claimed that she had been an unwilling accomplice to Bernardo's crimes, but videotapes shot by the couple proved otherwise.

and murder of Karla's 15-year-old sister, Tammy Lyn. The Canadian couple shared a seemingly insatiable appetite for sex and had no qualms when it came to fulfilling their sadistic fantasies.

Contrary to the claim made by Karla's lawyers – that she was an unwilling accomplice to the crimes – videotapes shot by the couple reveal that she was an active and enthusiastic participant, re-enacting Tammy Lyn's ordeal while dressed in her dead sister's clothes.

The press dubbed them the 'Ken and Barbie Killers', due to their similarity to the idealized toy dolls, but looks can be deceptive. Even the FBI profilers must have found it difficult to believe that this urbane, smart young man who would subsequently admit to a series of brutal sex murders was the serial rapist they had been hunting for six years.

Paul Bernardo is believed to have raped at least 19 underage girls in and around Scarborough, Ontario before he met his future wife. He claimed to have been the product of a violent home and blamed his brutal stepfather for sexually abusing his sister and alienating him from his mother, who withdrew from the family to live in the basement. But no one who met him in the late 1980s could imagine that he was anything other than an all-American college boy. Certainly not Karla Homolka.

Made for each other

Karla was the kind of girl every boy in her class dreamed of dating, but she was waiting for someone who would make her feel special, someone who would fulfil her secret fantasies. When 23-year-old Paul walked into the restaurant where she was having a late evening meal with a girlfriend, she must have thought her dreams had come true.

He was six feet tall, blond and had cultivated a smooth, affable manner that immediately put the girls at their ease. They invited him to join them and were impressed by his cool demeanour and his claim

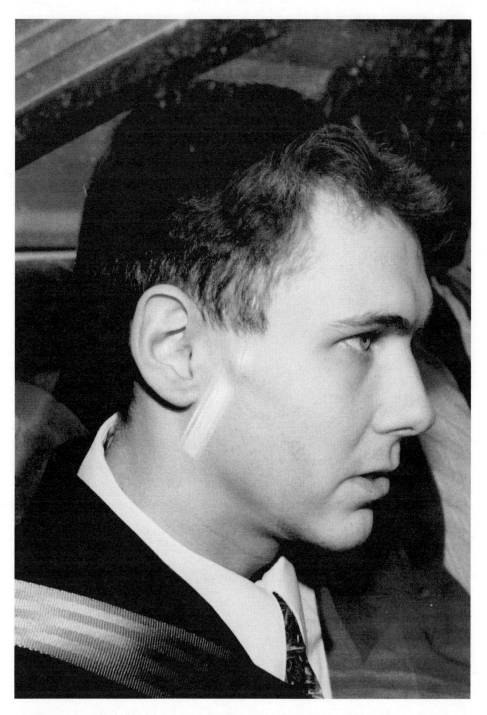

Bernardo leaves Metro East detention centre; he and his wife believed that they were too clever to be caught for their terrible crimes.

to have a well-paid job in a prestigious accountancy firm. He was going places and Karla wanted to be with him when he made a name for himself.

Paul sensed that she might be submissive and eager to please. He had an instinct for these things, having had a string of lovers whom he had manipulated into gratifying his sadistic desires, and he had high expectations that Karla might go further in fulfilling them than any of the others.

At first he reacted to her suggestive notes and her offer to be put in handcuffs as if it was as thrilling and daring for him as it seemed to be for her, but then he gradually increased his demands until she felt the only way to keep his interest was to submit. She had introduced him to her family and friends as her husband-to-be and she couldn't risk losing him by refusing to please him, no matter how degrading she might find it.

From there it was comparatively easy to persuade her to steal an anaesthetic from the veterinary practice where she worked and use it to drug her younger sister. Paul had been fantasizing about raping 15-year-old Tammy Lyn and by Christmas 1990 he had induced Karla to help him achieve it and to film the event for their subsequent stimulation. Unfortunately for them, Tammy choked on her own vomit and they had to convince the police that it had been an accident. Had the medical examiner suspected foul play and conducted a more thorough examination, he might have discovered sufficient evidence to prosecute the couple for sexual assault and manslaughter. But they had got away with murder and that only added to their belief that they were too clever to be caught.

The following summer they were married and Paul felt secure in the knowledge that a wife cannot testify against her husband. Paul subsequently abducted, raped and murdered 14-year-old Leslie

Mahaffy and 15-year-old Kirsten French with the active and willing participation of his wife, who videotaped the girls' ordeal.

Television appeal

In the summer of 1992, Special Agent Gregg O. McCrary agreed to appear on a local Canadian television channel and make a public appeal for information that might help the Toronto police catch a serial rapist who had recently graduated to murder. He offered a sketch of the killer based on the profile he had prepared for the police. The crimes, he told viewers, were 'high-risk, sexually motivated stranger homicides which are generally committed by men with a well-developed fantasy life which compels them to take greater risks and increases the chance of them making mistakes'.

Such men, he said, often begin with lewd behaviour and making obscene phone calls, before escalating to sexual assault, then rape and ultimately sadistic sexual murder.

'But although they are constantly on the prowl for potential victims, they will not act to fulfil their fantasy unless presented with an opportunity that is too good to miss or are pushed over the edge by a stressor – such as a fight with their partner.'

It was only after Paul Bernardo had turned on his partner in crime, his wife Karla, that the case came to its sordid conclusion.

Karla files assault charge

In January 1993 Karla filed an assault charge against her husband, who had battered her so badly with a torch that she had to be admitted to hospital. In her fury, her desire for revenge had overcome her common sense and she had summoned the police, forgetting for a moment that they were unlikely to arrest Paul and not make further enquiries into his background.

Perhaps she told herself that there was no risk in involving the police as they had been looking for two males in connection with the unsolved murders of Leslie Mahaffy in the summer of 1991 and Kirsten French in the spring of 1992. Sexual predators rarely work in pairs and when they do it is invariably two males. The murders had taken place across the border in neighbouring New York state whereas the rapes had occurred in Canada, so the police in both states were working on the assumption that the rapes and the murders were unrelated. In fact, Paul Bernardo had simply moved on to new hunting grounds and evolved from a rapist to a killer.

But astonishingly, he fitted both profiles.

Profiling a serial rapist

The report submitted to the Metropolitan Toronto Police on 17 November 1988 by Special Agents Gregg O. McCrary and James A. Wright stated:

> We do not believe the offender would attack a victim with a premeditated idea of murdering her. However, we would opine, based upon our research and experience, that if confronted by a victim who vigorously resists his attack, your offender is the type who would likely become so enraged he could lose control and thereby become capable of unintentionally murdering the victim.

After examining police reports the agents noted the escalating violence in the more recent attacks, which led them to assume that the UNSUB (unidentified subject) had developed sadistic tendencies.

He asked the seventh victim, should I kill you, thereby making her beg for her life. The sadist achieves gratification by the victim's response to his attempts to dominate and control her either physically or psychologically: by posing a question that made the victim beg for her life he is deriving pleasure.

The agents concluded:

> Your offender is a white male, 18 to 25 years of age. It should be cautioned that age is a difficult category to profile since an individual's behaviour is influenced by emotional and mental maturity, and not chronological age.
>
> The offender's anger towards women will be known by those individuals who are close to him. He will speak disparagingly of women in general conversation with associates.
>
> He is sexually experienced but his past relationships with women have been stormy and have ended badly. In all probability he has battered women he has been involved with in the past. He places the blame for all his failures on women.

Their assessment of Paul Bernardo's personality proved to be uncannily accurate.

> If he has a criminal record, it will be one of assaultive behaviour. The arrests will likely be for assault, disturbing the peace, resisting arrest, domestic disturbance, etc.

His aggressive behaviour would have surfaced during adolescence. His education background will be at the high school level with a record of discipline problems. He may have received counselling for his inability to get along with others, his aggressiveness, and/or substance abuse.

They concluded that the offender was single, intelligent but an academic under-achiever:

Your offender harbours no guilt or remorse for these crimes. He believes his anger is justified and, therefore, so are the resultant attacks. His only concern is being identified and apprehended.

Outrage at lenient sentence

DNA samples taken at the scenes of the rapes provided proof that Paul Bernardo was the rapist they had been looking for, but they did not place him at the scenes of the murders. The police would need a confession to convict him and Karla provided it.

The local police encouraged Karla to confide in them with regards to the assault and to provide details of previous instances of her husband's violent behaviour. It was only then that investigators from the Toronto Sex Crimes Unit approached Karla and encouraged her to tell them all she knew about the series of rapes committed in the area. She sensed that if she didn't cut a deal then she would go down with her husband and so she sought out a lawyer who might be able to secure her immunity in return for a full admission of her part in the killings.

Karla was denied immunity, but in July 1993 she was offered a 12-year sentence in exchange for a confession and cooperation in securing her husband's conviction. In September the following year, the full extent of her willing participation in the murders was revealed and there was public outrage at what was seen as a far too lenient sentence.

Paul had given his lawyer permission to enter his home and retrieve his 'personal effects' from a secret hiding place. These items included videotapes on which the couple had filmed the torture and killing of their victims. They were eventually turned over to the authorities.

Need to dominate

Paul Bernardo fitted the FBI profile of a sexual sadist. He had above average intelligence, but his abusive background had instilled in him the belief that men had a right to gratify their sexual urges regardless of their partner's feelings. After suffering years of neglect and mistreatment at the hands of his neurotic mother and abusive stepfather, he had developed a volatile temper and a craving for sadistic sex. He was believed to be a malignant narcissist who affected a pleasant and polite demeanour, but it was a facade.

Several former girlfriends described him as kind and considerate until he was sure of their devotion and then he would demand that they gratify his craving for rough sex. It became clear that he was only aroused when inflicting pain or making the girl fear for her life and then she experienced great difficulty in getting free of him. He needed to control, dominate and humiliate women to satisfy his fantasy of having the power of life and death over them. The ultimate act for a sexual sadist is murder and Paul Bernardo would not feel fully satisfied until he had committed the ultimate act of possession.

It was only when he met Karla, who appeared to have shared his sadistic impulses, that he fulfilled his fantasy of having an adoring admirer to witness his power over other women.

Groomed as an accomplice

They had met when she was just 17 and he was 23. She told detectives how he had groomed her to serve as his willing accomplice by forbidding her from visiting her family and forcing her to style her hair the way he liked it and dress in clothes he chose for her. He dismissed every objection with flattery, which overcame her resistance, but he cared nothing for her feelings. She was his fantasy woman, a living sex doll to be used and abused. He was incapable of empathy and derived pleasure from belittling her when she did something that displeased him, which frequently involved vain efforts to assert herself. Then he would criticize her until she gave in, but her willing compliance and dependency only made him more overbearing and in his eyes she became a mere object to be used and manipulated.

At least this is the way she portrayed herself to detectives, who must have wondered if it was all an act on her part after they found a number of true crime books in the house. From these she might have learned what to say if she wanted to appear to be the submissive, unwilling accomplice. They doubted her assertion that she had been isolated from her family and they were also suspicious of her story, which was told without any expression of guilt or remorse.

Sexual predators

Many women are confident that they would recognize the danger signs long before they became involved with a manipulative man, but a study of sadistic sexual predators by the FBI Behavioral Science Unit revealed that any woman could fall for the superficial charm of a psychopath.

Such men – and indeed women – rarely exhibit any outward signs of abnormality. They have developed the ability to appear as 'normal' and unthreatening as possible by studying and mimicking the behaviour of those around them. They have also become adept at 'reading' the personality of their intended victim, who will have no idea that they are being screened or assessed by means of the seemingly insignificant tell-tale signs and signals they give in their speech and body language. But a man like this will deliberately seek out vulnerable women and once he has seduced his victim with gifts, attention and affection he will exploit her longing for companionship and security. Step-by-step he will isolate her from her friends and family so that she will become entirely dependent on him.

He might convince her to reduce her social activities and meals with friends, so they can save enough money to buy a home together. If she agrees, he may increase her isolation by insisting that she cut down on telephone calls to her family. Once he feels that she is suggestible and entirely at his mercy, he can groom her to fulfil his fantasy by having her alter her appearance and perform sexual acts which will lower her self-esteem and make her feel that they share a guilty secret. Now she has lost all self-respect and is alienated from those to whom she might have turned for advice, she will continue to do whatever he asks because she is tormented by the possibility that he might tire of her and seek to gratify his desires with someone else.

She is now completely vulnerable and he can get her to do anything he desires – she will even become an accomplice to murder.

Claimed to be a victim

In May 1995 Paul Bernardo was found guilty on two counts of first-degree murder, two counts of kidnapping, two counts of sexual assault, two counts of forcible confinement and one count of committing an indignity to a human body. He was sentenced to life in prison with eligibility for parole in 2020.

At her trial Karla pleaded guilty to two counts of manslaughter, as had been agreed, and was sentenced to two consecutive ten-year terms, with an additional two years for her part in her sister's death. She was denied parole in 1997 and again in 2001, on the grounds that she was too dangerous to be released, but she was finally freed in 2005.

She claimed to have been a victim of her husband's abuse, but as agent McCrary commented in his summary of the case, the fact that she could kill her own sister and then continue to participate in more rapes and murders revealed a 'truly deviant personality'.

Mummy dearest – Fred and Rose West

In November 1995 a 41-year-old Gloucestershire housewife and mother was taken from the dock at Winchester Crown Court and bundled into a blacked-out police van. She was then driven to prison to begin ten consecutive life sentences for murder. Rosemary West, dowdy, bespectacled and overweight, looked as if she wouldn't have asserted herself at a church bazaar, but she and her husband Fred were responsible for some of the most horrific crimes to be tried in a British court.

As one reporter put it, she was no Myra Hindley – meaning that unlike Hindley she did not look anything like a sadistic sex-crazed killer. And yet West had actively and willingly participated in the abduction, torture and murder of ten women and girls, some of them her own children.

During the eight-week trial, some newspapers attempted to portray Rosemary West as being the dominant partner and her late husband (who had committed suicide before he had to face trial) as the 'moronic and doting' assistant. However, he was no subservient sidekick. He had killed before they met.

House of horrors

Twenty-eight years before the Cromwell Street murders hit the headlines, Fred West killed his children's nanny, Anne McFall, and probably also his first wife Rena, who went missing in the summer of 1967 and was never seen again. Anne's body was subsequently discovered buried in a field near to where Fred West had grown up. The autopsy revealed that Anne was carrying his unborn child. He had two young daughters at the time and the prospect of providing for a third child with his lover had evidently been the 'stressor' that tipped this volatile personality over the edge.

Fred and Rose West came to believe that incest and other deviant behaviours were absolutely normal.

Two years later, Fred met Rosemary Letts, who was then only 15 and a victim of rape and domestic violence. Her mother, brother and sisters had all been subjected to beatings meted out by their violent father. It is significant that she shared several characteristics with her future victims, who were all vulnerable teenagers from broken and abusive homes. It is as if she was 'kicking down', as bullies do; taking out her hatred on those in her care who were unable to defend themselves. Fred, on the other hand, actively sought out a partner to bolster his lack of confidence, to assure him that he was a 'real man' and to stave off his fear of inadequacy.

Rosemary claimed to have been raped twice by strangers before she moved in with Fred, who was then 27, and his two young daughters. They were sharing a dilapidated, crowded caravan in a trailer park when Rosemary became pregnant with the first of their ten children.

By the time they began picking up young girls and bringing them back for sex in the early 1970s, they were living as a family in a small house in Gloucester. According to criminal psychologists they must have been justifying their abuse by telling each other that their victims secretly enjoyed it. Their depravity came to a temporary halt in November 1970 when Fred was sent to prison for nine months, but during his absence Rosemary murdered her stepdaughter, seven-year-old Charmaine, in a fit of rage. On his release, the couple and their children moved to 25 Cromwell Street, where they established a boarding house which doubled as a brothel.

From April 1973 until May 1988, they were accused of murdering at least nine young women and girls and burying the bodies in the basement of the house and in the back garden. Among the remains, the police discovered the body of Fred and Rosemary's 16-year-old daughter Heather.

Victims were vulnerable

In each case it is thought that the victims were murdered to conceal the extent of the abuse they had suffered and were not killed for the perverse pleasure the couple derived from the act of killing. Their crimes were rooted in their inability to form healthy adult relationships and to see others as anything other than objects to be used to gratify their unrestrained and abnormal sexual needs. Being both unstable and chronically insecure, they sought out vulnerable and isolated individuals they could dominate, exercising power they did not have over others. In torturing their victims and then leaving them bound and gagged for days, they prolonged this delusion of power.

As Helena Kennedy QC observes in her book *Eve Was Framed*:

> On the few occasions when women have played a role in serial killings, as in the Moors and Manson murders, they have functioned as hand maidens to a master . . . Some women feel strangely flattered at being chosen by such men, as though they had been singled out from the ordinary run of womankind.

Evil begets evil

In this instance, it would appear that Rosemary and Fred's abnormal personalities were formed from birth. Rosemary's mother had been subjected to electroshock therapy for depression while she was pregnant. Perhaps as a result of this, when Rosemary was born in November 1953 she was regarded as being emotionally and mentally retarded. Her odd behaviour earned her the nickname 'Dozy Rosie'.

Her home life was violent and abusive, with her schizophrenic father taking out his frustrations on every member of the family, including his wife and little Rose.

Her brother Andrew later recalled:

> If he felt we were in bed too late, he would throw a bucket of cold water over us. He would order us to dig the garden, and that meant the whole garden. Then he would inspect it like an army officer, and if he was not satisfied, we would have to do it all over again. We were not allowed to speak and play like normal children. If we were noisy, he would go for us with a belt or chunk of wood. He would beat you black and blue until mum got in between us. Then she would get a good hiding.

All of her siblings would have been adversely affected by witnessing the beatings and living in an atmosphere of fear and despair. But while they presumably internalized their pain, Rosemary learned to vent her frustration by inflicting pain on others. Even while still a young girl she compensated for her sense of helplessness by exercising power and control over her younger siblings. She avoided some of the worst of the abuse by allying herself with her abusive father, in the same way that some prisoners often side with their jailers when they see no other means of alleviating their own suffering.

As a teenager Rosemary came to despise her mother for 'playing the victim', as she saw it, and she deliberately ramped up the level of abuse and violence that she used on her siblings and later on her own children and her vulnerable teenage victims. She seemed to be demonstrating to her absent father that she had become someone he might have approved of.

Monster in the making

Fred was one of six children raised by a Herefordshire farm labourer. His indulgent mother excused his antisocial behaviour as nothing more than high spirits and dismissed his compulsive lying as harmless fantasizing. He was in the habit of telling classmates and girls that he wanted to sleep with that he had made one of his sisters pregnant and that his father had sexually abused his own daughters. When the girls complained to their teachers, Fred's mother would defend him by saying that he had an overactive imagination and she repeatedly remonstrated with his headmaster when he caned the boy for his disruptive behaviour and insolence. But when her son graduated to petty theft, shoplifting and having sex with underage girls, his parents turned him out of the house.

At the age of 20 he narrowly avoided jail after being accused of the attempted rape of a 13-year-old by claiming that he suffered from seizures as the result of a serious motorbike accident, which had left him with a metal plate in his skull.

The accident, and a second fall from a fire escape during a sexual assault on an unwilling girl, appears to have made him more aggressive and he became a sexual predator, taking a job driving an ice cream van so that he could chat up young girls. He had an insatiable appetite for weird sex and paid for it when he couldn't get it for free. In 1962, he married a prostitute, Catherine (Rena) Costello, who was then pregnant with Charmaine, a child she had conceived with an Asian lover. Charmaine was dark-skinned, so Fred pretended that he and Rena had adopted the child.

They then had a child of their own, Anna Marie, but there was no likelihood of them settling down to a normal family life. First of all, Fred lost his job after a fatal accident in which a young boy was run over with his van. The odd couple then moved to Gloucester and there

Fred found a job in an abattoir, which satisfied his morbid obsession with blood, dismemberment and necrophilia.

Partners in depravity

Rena became increasingly disturbed by her husband's 'unnatural' sexual needs. After accusing him of being a pervert, she finally walked out. Despite her misgivings, she left both of her daughters in his care, presumably reassuring herself that his new lover, Anne McFall, would look after them. But Anne was to become his first victim, the first of a dozen or more women he is suspected of having murdered in the years before he met Rosemary Letts.

Rosemary's mother naively asked her daughter why a married man would be interested in befriending a 15-year-old girl, but Rosemary knew it was not companionship that Fred was after. He craved a willing partner in his perverse sexual games, a young girl who would do as she was told no matter how degrading the activity.

But Rosemary was not a passive partner. She had a vicious temper when aroused, as in the summer of 1971 when she murdered her step-daughter Charmaine and buried her under the kitchen floor. When asked to explain the child's absence, she claimed that her mother, Rena, had taken her back. For many years, Rosemary cooked and ate in that kitchen as if nothing had happened there, knowing that the decomposing corpse lay under her feet.

When the police recovered the remains in 1995, during an extensive excavation of the Wests' former home in Midland Road, they discovered that the girl's fingers and toes had been removed, a macabre ritual that was identified as being Fred's peculiar signature. He had mutilated Rena's body in the same way.

The family home was now an established brothel, where Rose entertained her clients while Fred watched through a peephole. The more degrading the act, the more Fred became aroused. And yet both felt the need to legitimize their relationship by marriage. In January 1972, they became husband and wife and six months later a daughter, Mae, was born.

With the addition to the family a move to a larger house was required, so they moved to 25 Cromwell Street that summer. Fred thought the cellar would make the perfect torture chamber. He said as much to a neighbour, who naturally assumed he was joking.

Raped own children

'Evil' is a word that is invariably used as an emotional response to an inhuman act of cruelty, when other terms seem inadequate to convey our revulsion. It expresses our disbelief that a human being could be so callous and lacking in compassion or conscience as to subject another person to systematic and repeated savagery. But this is precisely what Fred and Rosemary West did to their own children over many years.

They soundproofed the basement of their family home and there they subjected their eight-year-old daughter Anna Marie to repeated physical abuse. She was bound and gagged so that she would be powerless to resist being raped by her own father. He told her that he was only showing her how to satisfy her future husband and kept her away from school until the worst of her injuries began to heal.

Fred could not confine himself to sexually assaulting his own children. His next victim was the couple's 17-year-old nanny, Caroline Owens. She reported her rape to the police and Fred found himself in court. But despite his record of sexual offences, he walked free after the judge accepted his assurance that Caroline had consented.

Caroline's replacement, Lynda Gough, was silenced before she could report her experiences to the police. Lynda was murdered, dismembered and buried under the floor of the garage. None of the neighbours appear to have complained that these 'structural improvements' were being carried out after midnight.

Born into hell

Incredibly, none of the couple's subsequent victims appear to have sensed the danger that they were walking into, perhaps because they could not imagine that a family home would prove to be a trap. Fifteen-year-old Carol Ann Cooper was murdered in the house in November 1973 and so too was university student Lucy Partington, who was tortured for a week before she died of her injuries. Twenty-one-year-old Therese Siegenthaler, 15-year-old Shirley Hubbard and 18-year-old Juanita Mott were brutalized and abused before they too were killed.

Neither the school nor the social services appear to have taken a serious interest in the welfare of the West children, while those who expressed concern found themselves powerless to instigate an investigation without proof. Meanwhile the house in Cromwell Street was now home to more of the couple's hapless children and a number of lodgers, including 18-year-old prostitute Shirley Robinson. Bisexual Shirley was pregnant with Fred's child when she too was murdered and buried in the back garden. Rosemary had allegedly given her errant husband the order to get rid of the evidence of his infidelity. At the time, Rosemary was herself pregnant and gave birth to a daughter, Tara, in December 1977. The following year Rosemary produced their sixth child, Louise.

Three more children would be born in the early 1980s, just prior to the discovery that would put Cromwell Street on the murder map. And during that period more vulnerable teenagers would be lured to violent and terrible deaths in the basement of the family home.

But the couple could not intimidate their own children indefinitely. Their eldest offspring were now aware that they did not have to suffer

Fred and Rosemary West's former home at 25 Cromwell Street is prepared for demolition.

in silence – if they could summon the courage to go to the police and accuse their parents.

Search warrant obtained

Heather made the fatal mistake of confiding in a friend instead of reporting her parents to the police. But before her accusations could be investigated, she was murdered. Her parents claimed that she had left home to live with a boyfriend and that they had no idea of her whereabouts. They also attempted to discredit her as a witness by claiming that she was a drug addict given to fantasizing and that she could not be trusted.

It was not until August 1992 that the full extent of Fred and Rosemary's years of abuse and murder finally came to the attention of the authorities. Their latest victim, a young girl who had survived her ordeal, managed to blurt out her story to a friend, who in turn reported what she had been told to the police. A warrant was obtained, giving the detectives the authority to search the house.

Initially the investigation was centred on the couple's possession of child pornography. There was no suggestion at that time that the Wests had murdered their victims. But as a result of the search Fred was charged with the rape and sodomy of a minor and Rose was accused of being an accessory. The basement and garden could not be excavated until there was sufficient reason to assume that a body had been buried at the site. It was only after detectives failed to find any trace of Heather West that they were able to obtain a warrant to excavate her former home.

Human remains unearthed

On 24 February 1994 they began their search by demolishing the extension and digging up the back garden. Fred sensed that the game was up and confessed to murdering his daughter, Heather. But his compulsion to fantasize led him to recant and fabricate an even more improbable lie.

'Heather's alive and well,' he told his interrogators. 'She's possibly at the moment in Bahrain working for a drug cartel. She had a Mercedes, a chauffeur and a new birth certificate.'

However, when human remains were unearthed at the site he confessed again to having killed Heather. It was an accident, he told them. But as no one was likely to believe him he had dismembered her body in the bath tub and thrown the head and limbs into the dustbin. After dark he had buried the bags in the back garden. He had strangled her first, though, just to make sure she didn't recover consciousness while he was cutting her up.

'I didn't want to touch her while she was alive. If I'd have started cutting her leg or her throat and she'd have suddenly come alive . . . '

Heather's remains were among the 12 bodies recovered at the house: three in the garden and nine more in the cellar. Fred was suspected of killing many more, but he had lost count of whom he had murdered and when and where he had disposed of the bodies.

When detectives confronted Rosemary with his confession, she pretended to be completely surprised and horrified, but she was an equally poor liar.

Suicide in cell

On 13 December 1994, Frederick West was charged with 12 murders, but he didn't live to stand trial. He committed suicide in his cell on New Year's Day 1995.

Nine months later Rosemary West appeared in court and was forced to listen to the shocking testimony of her own daughter Anna Marie. But it was her own arrogance and angry outbursts from the dock which did as much to condemn her in the eyes of the jury.

Fred's taped confession was replayed in court, but few believed his repeated assertion that his wife was innocent. A decisive piece of evidence was the testimony of Janet Leach, an impartial civilian witness and part-time social worker who had sat in on Fred's interrogations. She told the court that he had agreed to take the blame for the deaths of Charmaine and Shirley Robinson, although Rosemary had committed the murders.

Rosemary West was convicted on all ten counts of murder and given a life sentence for each of them. The house at 25 Cromwell Street was subsequently demolished, but the traumatic effect on the West children and their parents' few surviving victims is incalculable. Perhaps the most unsettling aspect of the case was the fact that, despite the abuse they had suffered, some of the West children still felt an emotional attachment to their mother and father.

Air of normality

Neil McKay, author of *Appropriate Adult*, a TV drama based on the Fred West police interviews, identified the reason why the Cromwell Street killings have had such a profoundly unsettling impact on the public consciousness – they 'violate' our image of what a home should be, namely 'safe, secure and loving'. We are also disturbed by the fact that the Wests affected an air of normality, contrary to our image of what a serial killer couple should be like.

> ... though there was gossip about Rose's activities as a prostitute, the Wests were generally well-liked locally. Fred West especially was genial, affable and possessed of a beguiling charm which he used equally on men and women. If you look at photos of him cracking

the police up with laughter after his arrest you can
see this.

The Cromwell Street murders also had a profound and lasting effect
on those involved in the investigation. Among them was Janet Leach,
who McKay describes as 'an accidental witness' to the crimes.

When Janet Leach first met Fred West, she had no
idea who he was nor what he had done. She was a
housewife and part-time social-work student who
had recently gone on the appropriate adult register – a
list of persons approved to sit in on police interviews
with vulnerable people, in order to assist them and
safeguard their rights . . .

The police wanted to be sure that his legal defence
team could not later claim he had not understood the
proceedings. Within minutes of entering the interview
room she heard him describe the murder of his
daughter Heather in graphic detail . . .

As the interviews proceeded West began to
privately confide information about his crimes to
her, information which, because of obligations of
confidentiality, she was not free to pass on directly to
the police. West knew this and exploited the power this
gave him, both over her and the police. He rewarded
Leach – emotionally – for the moral support he
demanded from her if he was ever going to tell the
full truth. And if she had not given that support there
might have been families who, even now, might never
have found out what happened to their loved ones . . .

It is unimaginable to most of us how deviant individuals such as Fred and Rosemary West were able to live among the community and present themselves as outwardly normal citizens while subjecting their own children to mental and physical torture as well as sexually abusing them. Part of the reason why they were able to sustain this deception and live a double life for so long is because like so many aberrant personalities they only lost control when their authority was challenged.

Such people also make the fatal and tragic mistake of assuming that because they themselves do not value the life they were given, then neither do others. They are incapable of identifying with their victims and also lack the imagination to put themselves in the same situation.

Cannibal couple

Christmas is a time when many families gather together to give each other presents, overindulge in festive food and share the seasonal spirit. But not every family celebrates with the traditional turkey.

For Christmas dinner 1999 Russian couple Dmitry Baksheev and his wife Natalia served up a severed human head complete with stuffing and all the trimmings. It was one of the couple's first killings and they were evidently determined to celebrate in style.

The pair from Krasnodar in the Kirov region in southern Russia allegedly confessed to killing more than 30 people over the course of 20 years and cannibalizing their remains. They kept the choicest cuts in their fridge and cellar, stored pickled organs in jars and preserved other parts in a deep freeze. But their sickening crimes finally came to light after Natalia's stupid hubby took selfies with his lifeless victims, which he showed to colleagues at the military academy where he was employed as a cleaner.

Krasnodar as it looks today. Over the course of 20 years, Dmitry Baksheev and his wife killed and ate more than 30 people.

Instead of denying all knowledge of the murders, Dmitry boasted that he had been getting away with murder since 1999, though his motive remained unclear. During the interrogation it became evident that Natalia, who worked as a nurse, was the dominant personality and that the last victim, 35-year-old waitress Elena Vashrusheva, had been killed 'in a jealous rage after flirting with Dmitry'. Elena had been dismembered post-mortem and forensic experts subsequently identified her body parts as being among those pickled in a jar and stored in the couple's fridge.

Other victims would prove to be more difficult, if not impossible, to identify as there was little left of them other than what was described as 'steamed human meat'.

Killed to please wife

Many of their victims were believed to be unattached women who had been lured to their deaths by Dmitry, who had posed as a lonely single man on an online dating site. Tellingly, Dmitry had few complaints about his treatment at the hands of the Russian police, though he protested at being separated from his wife, as if her forceful and controlling presence provided him with the reason to live and the courage to commit his crimes. He admitted that their enforced separation during the trial and their subsequent imprisonment caused him great concern and that he had killed to please her.

Their relationship, he confessed, had been a 'mad' passionate affair, implying that he had become so infatuated with her that he had lost all sense of morality. This carried little weight with the prosecution, however, who argued that the pair had sustained their killing spree over the course of two years. Their crimes had been premeditated and their subsequent acts of cannibalism revealed the full extent of their aberrant personalities and insatiable bloodlust.

Natalia, in her turn, attempted to persuade the authorities that she felt for her husband 'as a mother does for her child'. Newspaper reports claimed that Natalia, a nurse by profession, baked pies using human remains and sold them to a local café, in a seeming act of bravado.

However, perhaps fearing that they might be victimized in prison by violent cell-mates, the couple later retracted their original statements and claimed to be outraged at being called cannibals by the press! Unfortunately for them, an official police video taken inside their chaotically disordered apartment showed instructional videos on the subject of cannibalism.

If their dustbin of an apartment was symptomatic of their mental state, it is perhaps no surprise that they could no longer function as human beings. Which leaves only one question remaining – what did they serve for dessert?

Causes of abnormal behaviour

Although the cases described in the previous pages seem, on the surface at least, to have little in common, many reveal recurring patterns and provide insights into what causes such abnormal behaviour. Even those who commit apparently 'motiveless' murders have their reasons, although they are unlikely to be conscious of what triggers them.

Chief among these is the need to be recognized as being significant and having value, even if it is negative value, or notoriety. The psychologist Alfred Adler proposed the theory that human beings see life as a continual struggle to overcome feelings of inferiority and feel compelled to assert themselves in what they perceive to be a hostile, competitive world.

On an overpopulated planet, individuals who do not distinguish themselves are anonymous and dispensable in the eyes of society. Most of us learn to accept this and find satisfaction and a reason for living in personal achievements and the company of like-minded friends who provide moral and emotional support. However, sociopaths and psychopaths are, for one reason or another, incapable of accepting that they might be 'unexceptional' and actively seek to assert themselves and establish their imagined superiority. They set themselves above others and view the conformist with contempt. More often than not, they choose the crime with the least risk to themselves. If they evade detection, they are likely to intensify their pattern of antisocial or criminal behaviour until it provides them with the ultimate thrill. Murder is the last logical step in their escalating spiral of violence.

Partners in crime

If the perpetrator has coerced a partner into helping them, the less dominant partner is likely to have been someone who has been emotionally scarred by witnessing a traumatic incident or who has suffered abuse themselves. They will be more easily manipulated into killing, an act which forces them to face their fear of pain and death and overcome it with the encouragement and approval of a more forcible personality.

Without a willing, adoring disciple to witness the deed the dominant partner is likely to remain a frustrated fantasist. The less dominant partner invariably has no particular aspirations or drive. They drift through life lacking direction, daydreaming of meeting someone who will bring meaning to their life. When they find this person, who is also someone with a more forceful will, they tend to idolize them and are drawn into an increasingly subservient role. They find they can only channel their own energy and aggression through activities which the other has planned. They are what the Hungarian hypnosis specialist Ferenc Völgyesi termed 'psycho-passive' or easily influenced.

If, as has been suggested, we possess two minds – the objective which deals with external practical problems and the subjective which relates to introspective aspects located in the left and right cerebral hemispheres of the brain – then the dominant partner could be said to assume the role of the 'objective mind' and their partner the 'subjective'. The submissive partner slavishly obeys the dominant partner as if under hypnotic suggestion. In such a state, submissive partners blot out reality and are no longer responsible for their actions, assuming no responsibility. They are in a dissociative state.

Upping their game

The existence of so many partners in crime, particularly in families where the parents, partners or siblings are rivals for dominance, explains how one or more members of that family have exercised an almost hypnotic control over their less dominant partners and accomplices. As Wilson notes, the uncommon combination of high- and medium-dominance personalities often triggers the violence, which sees the dominant partner manipulating the less dominant partner into participating in criminal acts and cruelty they would not have committed had they not been under the influence of the stronger personality.

The primary partner is encouraged into upping their 'game' by this demonstration of unquestioning obedience. This is an entirely different dynamic than that exemplified by dominant and submissive partners. Moderately dominant personalities do not see themselves as victims but as valued accomplices. Their own craving for recognition and power is satisfied by serving an even more aggressive or forceful partner.

The Dark Web

The anonymity offered by the internet and the unrestricted access it provides to graphic, illicit images has provided unprecedented opportunities for those who would profit from the sale of hardcore pornographic material, drugs and even human beings. This virtual black market is known as the Dark Web and its potential for encouraging criminal activity and the exploitation of vulnerable individuals is surely the most alarming development of the digital age.

In August 2018, a German couple were convicted of selling their own son to paedophiles using the internet and each was sentenced to 12 years in prison. The pair, whose identities were withheld for legal reasons, were accused of having sexually assaulted the boy (who was nine when the trial began) for several years. Six males were also facing prosecution for their part in the abuse. Prosecutors claimed that the boy had been subjected to a total of around 60 serious attacks. Other charges against the couple related to forced prostitution, the sale of pornographic images and rape.

In addition to their sentence the couple were ordered to pay a substantial sum in compensation, both to the boy and a three-year-old girl, who was also said to have been abused.

The boy was committed into the care of foster parents.

Authorities failed to act

According to press reports, the mother's conviction for paedophilia was known to the authorities, who failed to act because they apparently found it hard to believe that a mother was capable of sexually abusing her own child. Not only was she accused of having done so repeatedly but she also allowed others to do so too, profiting financially from prostituting the boy and even participating in the filming of the abuse.

At one point social workers had removed the child, only to return him to his mother and stepfather because they mistakenly believed that they had insufficient grounds to put the boy into permanent care. Welfare officers had not shared information on the couple and so were not fully informed of their previous convictions and the concerns highlighted by an earlier investigation.

Chapter Five:
Crime Families

The myth of Ma Barker

The withered fingers of spidery, crafty Ma Barker, like Satanic tentacles controlled the skeins on which dangled the fate of desperadoes whose activities hit the headlines on an average of once a week.

King Features Syndicate press feature, 1935

On the afternoon of 15 January 1935 J. Edgar Hoover, director of the FBI, addressed a press conference in Washington, DC. He knew that the reporters were eager to hear which of America's public enemies had been captured or killed, so that they could satisfy their readers' insatiable appetite for news. The trouble was that the Barker–Karpis Gang were no headline grabbers. They were a hillbilly outfit and lacked a charismatic leader like John Dillinger or Pretty Boy Floyd.

At dawn that morning, after a lengthy shoot-out in Ocklawaha, Florida, the G-men had entered the Barker lakeside home to find two bodies – 63-year-old Kate Barker and her 34-year-old son Fred – lying side by side in a first-floor bedroom. Kate had been killed with a single bullet to the head, possibly self-inflicted. Fred had been running from room to room and firing from the windows to give the agents the impression that the whole gang were in there and were armed to the teeth, but there were no other gang members in the house. It was a poor haul and Hoover had to make the most of it. He also had to justify the killing of a grandmother with no criminal record.

So he lied. He told the journalists that Ma Barker was the 'evil' mastermind behind a spate of robberies, abductions and random killings and that she had refused an offer to surrender. Instead, she had ordered Fred to open fire on the agents with a machine gun and had died with a smoking Tommy gun in her hand.

If any of the newsmen had sought verification of Hoover's claims they would have discovered that there was no evidence to connect Kate Barker with any of the robberies Fred and the gang had carried out, other than the fact that she had spent a share of the proceeds buying groceries. It has been suggested that she took no active part in the planning and execution of their crimes and that her part was restricted to renting the houses in which the gang hid out after each job and providing them with provisions. A former criminal associate,

Ozarks crime matriarch Ma Barker, circa 1930.

Harvey Bailey, claimed that Kate Barker 'couldn't plan breakfast, let alone a robbery'.

'An old-fashioned homebody'

Alvin Karpis, the real leader of the gang, insisted that she was

> an old-fashioned homebody from the Ozarks; superstitious, gullible, simple, cantankerous and, well, generally law-abiding . . . She wasn't a leader of criminals or even a criminal herself. There is not one police photograph of her or set of fingerprints taken while she was alive . . . she knew we were criminals but her participation in our careers was limited to one function: when we travelled together, we moved as a mother and her sons. What could look more innocent?

Moreover, there was no indication that she had ever fired a gun, or knew one end of a machine gun from the other. Ma Barker was no saint, but there was nothing to support Hoover's claim that his men had ended the reign of an evil woman and her sons – the weak men she had coerced into a life of crime.

When the story failed to generate the kind of reaction Hoover was hoping for, he arranged for a multi-part feature entitled 'Ma Barker: Deadly Spider Woman' to be circulated to all the major newspapers in the country. The largely fictitious feature demonized Kate Barker and helped to disseminate the myth which has persisted to this day.

It also served to promote Hoover's obsession – the decline of moral values in America. This came from a man who is alleged to have led a secret life as a cross-dresser and closet homosexual while publicly condemning those who were caught doing the same.

FBI men gather outside the bungalow in Ocklawaha, Florida where Fred and Ma Barker died after a four-hour gun battle.

Career criminals became Hoover's mania, not only for the prestige and power their capture or death brought to the bureau, but also as a convenient focus for his own self-loathing and guilt. He would recount the story of the Barker gang at every opportunity, seeing in it a symbol of the moral decay at the heart of American society.

'She was so smart,' he would say, 'that we never got anything on her. We had to kill her to catch up with her.'

The Messina brothers

We Messinas are more powerful than the British Government. We do as we like.

Attilio Messina

It is said that there is 'no honour among thieves'. Just when a gang thinks itself invincible, a gang member will turn on the others and cut a deal with the law to save his own skin. One way to reduce the risk of being betrayed is to trust no one but your own flesh and blood and to exclude outsiders.

The Messina brothers [see also photo on page 11] , who controlled prostitution and gambling in London's West End from the mid-1930s until their arrest in the late 1950s, owed their prolonged reign to that philosophy. They became so powerful that they were able to boast of having the police in their pocket and it is said that they got away with murder – more than once.

The slaying of three prostitutes in Soho, London's red-light district, was attributed to the five brothers, who were believed to dispatch their 'working girls' in a way that would send a message to the other streetwalkers not to talk. One was stabbed in the stomach, so she wouldn't 'spill her guts' to the police, another had her eyes gouged out so that she couldn't tell what she had seen and a third had her tongue cut out so that she couldn't talk.

The five brothers, Alfredo, Attilio, Eugenio, Carmelo and Salvatore, who were all Italian-born but raised in Malta, controlled three dozen brothels catering for the poorest punter to the more affluent clients in Mayfair.

Their father, Giuseppe, had educated them in the sex trade business and when Eugenio emigrated to England in 1934 he put what he had learned into practice using his wife, a French prostitute, to recruit the girls. Girls were imported from Spain, Belgium and France and forced to surrender their passports so that they were at the mercy of their pimps. But whenever the police attempted to deport them, the girls' passports were produced, ensuring that they had a right to stay in the country.

Later the brothers lured innocent young women from the provinces into prostitution by contriving 'chance' meetings at railway stations and promising to show the naïve young visitors the big city. Before they woke up to the reality, the girls were committed to helping out their new Italian boyfriend by being 'extra nice' to his 'boss' or 'best friend', who was only later revealed to be a client.

Mystery deaths

The police believed that the brothers controlled 200 of the most exclusive call girls in London at the time and that they took the lion's share of their earnings: perhaps as much as 80 per cent. If they had restricted themselves to pimping, they might have been able to retire on their ill-gotten gains, which were estimated at £1,000 a week (around £20,000/$25,000 today), but they made the fatal mistake of enforcing their hold over the girls with violence.

Inspired by the misdeeds of the Messina brothers, the British B movie The Flesh is Weak *(1957) was an attempt to tackle the issue of prostitutes and the pimps who controlled them.*

Forty-one-year-old Rachel Fennick, known on the street as 'Ginger Rae', was found dead in her Soho flat on 26 September 1948. She had been stabbed once in the abdomen with a curved blade, most likely a Sphairhai, a 'Mediterranean' knife capable of gutting the victim with one upward thrust. She was the third of the Messina 'girls' to die a violent death, the others being 'Russian Dora' and 'Black Rita' (the six-foot-tall daughter of a former Bow Street police officer). All three murders went unsolved because it was alleged that detectives were paid to attribute the killings to anonymous clients who had vanished, leaving no clues at the scene.

Predictably, few of the girls were willing to talk to the police, who they believed were simply not interested in what happened to prostitutes at a time when soliciting for sex was illegal in Britain. There were rumours too that the police couldn't be trusted, that certain officers had taken bribes from the Messinas to look the other way when there was trouble. But one man was determined to bring the brothers down and dispel the fear that permeated London's red-light district. He also had a nose for a good story when he heard one and could imagine the front-page headlines with his name in large bold type underneath.

Fearless reporter

Duncan Webb was still in his early thirties, but he had a reputation for ferreting out the truth and was already known as 'The Greatest Crime Reporter of Our Time', an appellation he was keen to live up to. He wouldn't be intimidated by the Messinas, or their strong-arm thugs, because he had survived beatings from the best. *Time* magazine reported that Webb had been 'slugged, kicked, lunged at with knives, shot at, knuckledusted and was once the target of a speeding automobile that raced on to the side-walk of a narrow Soho street and tried to smash him against a building'.

British gangster Billy Hill signs a copy of his autobiography in 1953 as crime journalist Duncan Webb, in glasses, looks on.

His employer, the *Sunday People*, had a healthy circulation of over five million and a readership with an insatiable appetite for sensational stories. 'If it bleeds, it leads' was the maxim of the newsroom, which meant that crime stories had priority over all other news. There were no secret payments to informants, but some villains talked freely to Webb over a pint in the saloon bar because they wanted to even the score with a rival and they trusted him not to name his sources. One such figure was Billy Hill, whose rival, Jack Spot, was belittled by Webb in one article as a 'tinpot dictator'. Spot had earlier broken Webb's arm in one of several attacks the reporter had suffered in pursuit of a scoop. It was Billy's boys who protected Webb when the Epsom Salts, as the East End gangsters called the Maltese, came looking to 'do him proper'.

'They know I cannot be bought or sold, nor is there a lot of which I am afraid.'

Obtaining the evidence

Cracking the Messinas was another matter though, as everyone was too frightened to talk. But Webb was persistent. He began by publishing a series of articles accusing an unnamed member of the Vice Squad of tipping off the brothers whenever there was to be a raid on one of their brothels or other joints. Having shown his courage in accusing the law of collusion and corruption, the girls gradually opened up to him, one even offering to give him a 'free sample' if he could introduce her to a male movie star. The reporter politely declined.

Webb was too well known in Soho to make the initial approach to the girls, so he persuaded his assistant Murray Sayle, an Australian, to pose as a punter. Once inside the girls' flat, Murray had to elicit a verbal offer of sex in exchange for money in order to have the necessary proof that the girl was a prostitute and that the flat was being used for immoral purposes. For reasons too complicated to go into, she also had to be in a state of undress at the time, while Murray remained fully clothed. At that stage Murray was to extricate himself, which gave rise to the famous phrase: 'At which point I made my excuses and left.' It was then simply a matter of obtaining documentary evidence linking the Messinas to that address.

Webb was audacious, but he was also thorough. By the end of his three-month, one-man investigation into the Messinas' sordid business empire he had amassed more than a hundred interviews detailing crucial names, dates and addresses of brothels owned by the brothers, information that he could then pass on to Scotland Yard. But not before he had written a real 'marmalade dropper' of a story (so called because it would cause the reader to drop their morning toast in disbelief), which exposed the brothers as vicious thugs.

The power of the press

The headline on 3 September 1950 ran 'Arrest These Four Men', under which Webb described the Messina brothers as 'four debased men with an empire of vice which is a disgrace to London'. It was a challenge to both the Met and the Messinas to prove the charges were false, but all the evidence against the gang was there in black and white. The newspaper challenged the brothers to sue for libel, knowing that they wouldn't dare. Until then, the brothers had relied on the fact that the word of a prostitute would be worthless in court, but the court of public opinion was something else and the police were effectively shamed into acting on the evidence Webb had collected. But they only acted after the paper had run seven more front-page exposés and questions had been asked in the Houses of Parliament concerning the seeming reluctance of the police to arrest what Webb had dubbed 'this vile gang'. (Webb's initial frustration with

Eugenio Messina sticks out his tongue at photographers as he is led into court in Belgium to face charges of procuring women, illegal possession of firearms, possession of fake passports and entering the country illegally; meanwhile, his brother Carmelo shields his face with his hand behind the double door.

the tardiness of the police investigation was expressed by the wording of a personal advertisement he placed in *The Times*, giving thanks to St Jude, the patron saint of lost causes.)

Alfredo and Attilio were arrested, convicted and sentenced to two years in prison for living off immoral earnings. In addition, Alfredo was charged with attempting to bribe the officer who arrested him. The gangster brothers fled the country in March 1951, with Eugenio and Carmelo decamping in a yellow Rolls-Royce. Their criminal empire had been brought down, the pen for once having proven mightier than the sword.

The five Messinas, however, continued to profit from vice using a Corsican associate, Antonio 'Tony' Rossi, who sent their illicit earnings to them in France, via a courier, well into the 1950s.

But the Messinas were no longer a presence in London and in response to the public outcry over their activities parliament passed the Sexual Offences Act in 1959, which criminalized any property being used for prostitution.

Legends?

> [My boys] are the most understanding and kindest
> of people one could meet and they have never hurt
> anyone, only their own kind.
>
> *Undated letter from Violet Kray to a friend*

The Kray Twins, Ronnie and Reggie, are inextricably linked in the public consciousness with the 'Swinging Sixties' and as a result the more brutal aspects of their criminal activities have been conveniently glossed over so as not to taint the collective memory. But the fact remains that the 'boys' had an unpleasant habit of enforcing their grip on London's underworld with gratuitous violence and cruelty. Reggie's favourite was the 'cigarette punch', which he used when offering the victim a cigarette. He'd catch them with their guard down and their mouth open, which frequently left the recipient with a fractured jaw.

The Krays cultivated an image of the decent thug who kept their own kind in line and the streets safe for law-abiding locals. There is more than a hint of racism in the determination of some older East End residents to see the twins as strong, self-made men who clawed their way out of post-war poverty but never forgot their roots and their assertation that the Krays were preferable to the gangs of youths they now blame for making East End estates frightening places to live.

Like Hitler, the Krays idolized their mother and loved their dog. They sided with their mother against their enfeebled father and were doted on by their grandmother, Mary Lee, and two aunts, Rose and May. According to biographer John Pearson, their dependency on these hard-working but overindulgent women contributed to their sexuality, which was apparently compounded by their mother's insistence on dressing them in girls' clothes when they were small. Reggie was believed to be bisexual and Ronnie gay and if the prison psychiatrists are correct, the repression of their sexual preferences in the assertive, misogynistic culture of post-war Britain would account for their overly macho posturing and predisposition to sadistic violence.

They seemed to many to symbolize the indomitable, defiant wartime community spirit when the East End took the brunt of German bombs and carried on regardless. But if the Krays played up to that, they were really only looking after their own interests. And the more profitable these were, the more ruthless the 'boys' were in enforcing their claim.

Amateur boxers Reggie (left) and Ronnie Kray with their mother Violet back in 1950. Those two boys loved their mum.

However, their crude armoury was decidedly 'old school' compared to the high-tech weaponry sported by today's criminals. They had knuckledusters, an old army bayonet, a crossbow, a sawn-off shotgun and even a child's catapult, which may have had sentimental attachments.

'We've not been angels'

When Pearson met the Krays in the autumn of 1967 – which became commonly known as the Summer of Love – his initial impression was that the twins called the shots and their seemingly ill-at-ease elder sibling, Charlie, sat on the sidelines urging them on.

Ronnie was everything the writer had imagined an East End hood to be like. 'He had a slow, faintly sneering way of speaking that sounded threatening even when it wasn't and his eyes bulged too much for comfort.' He looked, in his biographer's words, 'permanently nasty'.

Though they were frequently referred to as 'identical twins', no one could have mistaken one for the other. Reggie, according to Pearson, was 'very different – thinner, quicker, with a certain shifty charm'. It was this veneer of 'boyish' charm that fooled so many people until they got on the wrong side of the Krays' temper. When Pearson met them, Reggie was still sporting a bandaged hand, cut in the 'heated discussion' that only weeks before had left enforcer Jack 'The Hat' McVitie fatally wounded after being invited to a 'house party' in Stoke Newington. McVitie would have met a quicker, cleaner end had Reggie's gun not jammed, which left the latter no choice but to stab McVitie repeatedly in the face, chest and stomach. When Pearson asked him how he had hurt his hand in an effort to break the ice on their first meeting, Reggie answered curtly: 'Gardening.'

With Detective Chief Superintendent Leonard 'Nipper' Read of the Met murder squad breathing down their necks and reports that one of their own had turned 'supergrass' to save his own skin, the twins were seriously considering 'retirement' that heady summer. But before they were banged up for life, they wanted to tell their side of the story to someone they could be sure wouldn't embellish it.

'So much rubbish gets written about our sort of people,' said Reggie in his rapid monotone, 'that both me an' Ron think it's time the truth was told for once. We've not been angels,' he added with classic understatement, 'but we've done some interesting things and met some interesting people.'

Rise and fall of The Firm

The twins were born ten minutes apart on the morning of 24 October 1933 in Hoxton, east London. Their parents, Violet and Charles Snr, were a poor, working-class couple who scraped a meagre living selling old clothes and second-hand furniture. When Charles was unable to provide for his family, which included the twins' older brother Charlie Jnr, Violet was reduced to pawning her wedding ring.

When the boys were six, their father went on the run to avoid being conscripted into the army and their mother was forced to raise them with the help of their maternal grandfather, Jimmy 'Cannonball' Lee. It was Jimmy who attempted to channel their anger at being abandoned into something constructive, by encouraging them to take up boxing. It was a sport at which they excelled, to the extent that they turned professional while still in their teens.

But when they were 'called up' to serve their compulsory National Service in 1952, they absconded from the barracks after Ronnie floored an NCO. He then compounded the felony by punching a police constable who attempted to arrest them. It earned them the dubious distinction of being among the last prisoners to be held in the Tower of London, as well as a court martial, a spell in the glasshouse

The Kray twins were born in Hoxton, east London, traditionally a poor working-class area, which is currently undergoing gentrification.

and finally a dishonourable discharge for violent behaviour during their incarceration.

But it meant they were now free to pursue their chosen career – a life of crime.

They began the long haul up the ladder by extorting money from small businesses, committing arson to claim the insurance and hijacking goods which they resold to fences and through the black market, all the while backing their plays with muscle and intimidation. They invested their ill-gotten gains in a snooker hall in Mile End and a string of nightclubs, so that by the end of the 1950s 'The Firm', as the Krays liked to call themselves, had established itself as an outfit that was not to be messed with.

As their influence increased and their empire grew, they moved uptown and upmarket, expanding their activities into London's West End with assistance from legitimate as well as criminal contacts and attracting showbiz celebrities who performed at their clubs and used the services of their bodyguards.

The untouchables

> Me and my brother ruled London. We were fucking untouchable.
>
> *Ronnie Kray*

They had good reason to believe they were the Teflon twins. No newspaper would dare to print the truth about them, or expose their links to pillars of the British Establishment, after the *Sunday Mirror* published accusations of Ronnie's relationship with Conservative MP Lord Boothby in July 1964. Although the paper was careful not to name names, readers could read between the lines. Boothby subsequently sued the tabloid and won a substantial sum in damages with the aid of cross-party support from the Labour Party, who were concerned to protect the reputation of one of their openly gay MPs. The publishers were also pressured to sack the editor and print an apology to Boothby, who would not only have lost his membership of the House of Lords but might have faced criminal prosecution as homosexuality was still illegal at the time.

With the press and politicians gagged, the only threat to The Firm came from informers and witnesses, but these too were neutered by intimidation and the Krays' formidable reputation for savage retribution.

If it's true that you can judge people by the company they keep, then the Krays certainly kept some very dubious company. One of them was a notorious slum landlord, described by their biographer as 'a specialist in high-grade arson', who collected 'a quite extraordinary amount of money from a number of insurance companies on a series of large country houses which went up in smoke'. They evidently saw themselves as latter-day Al Capones who were sometimes grudgingly forced to beat some sense into anyone threatening what they coyly referred to as their 'way of life'.

A former gang member, Chris Lambrianou, admitted: 'Back in the day we looked up to gangsters like Dillinger, Al Capone, Legs Diamond, Bonnie and Clyde – that was what they fed us on, the American films, and I think the British press wanted something like that in this country.'

The Richardsons

Their rivals, Eddie and Charlie Richardson, retained their animosity towards the Krays into the new millennium, with Eddie accusing the twins of watching 'too many US gangster films'. 'They wanted to be Al Capone,' he taunted, reopening festering wounds that hadn't healed after 50 years, adding: 'They just wanted to play at being gangsters. They didn't dare take us on until we were under lock and key – then they started taking liberties.'

Eddie accused Ronnie and Reggie of lacking the brains to be big time criminals. 'They weren't in our league,' he sneered.

The Richardson gang used a scrap metal merchant's and a slot machine company as a front to launder money from their protection racket and other illegal enterprises in south London, a safe distance from the Krays' criminal interests in the East End. But there was no love lost between them and little respect. The Richardsons considered themselves the real deal and saw the Krays as poseurs. Eddie and Charlie savoured their well-earned reputation for violence, which had brought them the nickname 'the torture gang'. Those found guilty of creaming a bit off the top, or betraying them, were subjected to Gestapo tactics which included nailing their hands and feet to the floor, pulling out their teeth with pliers and applying electric shocks to their nipples and private parts.

The uneasy truce came to an end on 7 March 1966 when Kray associate Richard Hart came off worst in a brawl between the Richardson gang and the brothers at a south London club. Hart was shot in the face and died from his wounds. No one was convicted of his murder, but the Richardsons' enforcer, 'Mad' Frankie Fraser, was subsequently sentenced to five years for his part in the fight that led to Hart's demise.

It was the death of Hart that led directly to Ronnie Kray's slaying of the Richardsons' right-hand man, George Cornell, the next day. Ronnie walked free from custody when witnesses refused to testify, but the Richardsons were not so fortunate.

The day England celebrated its team's World Cup win over Germany, the Richardsons were arrested and their reign of terror came to an end.

Charlie was sentenced to 25 years for assault, extortion, fraud and GBH and Eddie was sent down for 15 years.

Gangster Charlie Richardson (second right) and Eddie Richardson (third right, holding face) weren't shy of flaunting their wealth in public.

John McVicar, former armed robber and serial escapist turned writer, once wrote:

Outsiders often think prisons are full of evil people. They're not. There are a lot of bad people locked up, but most are bad in a conventional way. They just do what those around them do; they mimic what the people they have fallen in with do. Evil people are probably as rare as truly saintly people.

Tweedledum and Tweedledee

The twins were self-serving, ruthless and murdering bullies.

Metropolitan Police sergeant Ken German

The Krays could be generous hosts and surprisingly entertaining storytellers, though they had to be careful what they divulged. No one was allowed to get too close. Ronnie's paranoia only manifested itself when he learned that former members of 'The Firm' were spilling their guts to 'that flash bastard copper' who had made it a personal crusade to put them out of circulation – Nipper Read of Scotland Yard. They'd named their pet boa constrictor after their nemesis and left it in the care of their old mum, who still lived in a block of council flats in Shoreditch, overlooking the city that her 'boys' boasted they owned.

It was only after they were securely locked away that journalists could risk calling them 'Gangland's Tweedledum and Tweedledee'.

Although their older brother Charlie was a member of 'The Firm', he kept a low profile after serving a stretch for being an accomplice in the McVitie murder and it wasn't until 1997 that he was convicted for his part in a £39 million cocaine smuggling operation and jailed for 12 years at the age of 70.

Ronnie died of a heart attack in Broadmoor on 17 March 1995 aged 61 and Reggie of bladder cancer on 1 October 2000 aged 66. Their black marble gravestone in Chingford Mount Cemetery features David Bailey's famous photo of the twins at the peak of their notoriety, attired in dark suits, white shirts and skinny ties.

But two other headstones in the same graveyard contradicted this glamorous image. One is that of their mother Violet, a forbidding personality who died in August 1982 and whose rose-tinted picture of her 'lovely boys' was never shattered by reality. The other is that of Reggie's emotionally unstable young wife Frances, who committed suicide by taking an overdose of sleeping pills on 7 June 1967, two years after their marriage. Her mother had a presentiment that it would end in tears, so she attended the wedding dressed in mourning black. After their daughter's death, Frances' parents tried in vain to have the grave moved in order to distance their daughter from the men who had ruined their lives and taken the life of their child.

Face to face with the Krays

In the 1980s, *Daily Mail* reporter Paul Callan interviewed Ronnie and Reggie in prison and recorded their chilling confessions of torture, intimidation and murder.

Ronnie took a perverse pleasure in reliving every detail of the night he 'done' East End gangster George Cornell for calling him 'a big fat poof'. As Ronnie walked blithely into the bar of The Blind Beggar on 9 March 1966, Cornell couldn't resist taunting him with one final insult.

'Look what the dog dragged in,' he said. They were the last words he uttered in his short and sordid life.

Ronnie pulled out a German Luger and shot Cornell in the head. 'I done the earth a favour,' he told the *Mail* reporter, the memory of that night momentarily assuaging the numbing boredom of nearly 20 years behind bars in Broadmoor.

Ronnie was just two years short of 50 when he granted Callan an interview and it was clear that he needed to relive his 'glory days' as much as the reporter needed the story. He craved attention, recognition and the misguided 'respect' that fear engendered in those who looked into his lifeless eyes and met that hard, unflinching stare across the table in the visitors' room.

Broadmoor was a forbidding Victorian psychiatric hospital whose inmates were not there for their health. Ronnie had been diagnosed as a dangerous schizophrenic and a psychopathic personality. He shared a wing with Ian Brady, the Moors Murderer, and the pair would cook for their fellow inmates and pass the tedious hours imagining that the outside world was still morbidly obsessed by their crimes.

In Ronnie's case his egomania had been fed and flattered by a never-ending series of books on the brothers' life and crimes and the certainty that the public's interest in him would continue with the release of a number of films glamorizing their rise and fall. He also took pride in reeling off the list of celebrities who had come to visit him: Judy Garland, Diana Dors, the boxer John Conteh and the actors James Fox and Richard Burton, both of whom came to Broadmoor to pick up tips on how to portray a hard man on screen.

All were names from the past whose fame he desperately needed to see aligned with his own notoriety. In his mind, their interest was confirmation of his 'legendary' status. Without these fleeting 'endorsements' he would be just another dangerous psychopath who needed to be caged to keep society safe.

As Callan noted:

> The very fact that I was writing down Ronnie's observations appeared to please him. It gave him a sense of importance and when another 'patient' (as prisoners are called at Broadmoor) approached us, Ronnie waved him away.
>
> 'I'm being interviewed by the *Daily Mirror*,' he said. 'Don't bother us just now.'

Hearts of gold

The Krays were acutely conscious of their public image and went out of their way to foster the picture of themselves as local hoodlums with hearts of gold. They made generous donations to local youth clubs and paid for pensioners' teas at a Bethnal Green café to cement their 'legend' as local heroes.

Ronnie was immaculately groomed for the interview with Callan, his long, pointed face 'scrubbed', his raven hair slicked back and his fingernails newly manicured. He was passing the time painting and listening to opera and now saw himself as an artist. At the end, he even offered to send the reporter a landscape.

He admitted to having suffered depression when he was sent down for life without parole in 1969 for the killing of rival hard men George Cornell and Jack McVitie, but had now learned to 'take it easy' and alleviate the tedium with exercise, particularly walking. 'But not right out of the gate,' he added, with the faint trace of a smile. Then his expression hardened and he voiced the resentment that had been seething inside him.

'I understand to a point why I've got to do a long time in prison. But not my brother. Not Reggie. He never done no murders. I done them. Reg is innocent.'

He still believed in his own myth, that of the 'honourable gangster'.

'We never harmed no one on the outside. No "civilians". We kept to our own people.'

There was the inevitable note of self-pity for having been caught and then being forced to face the consequences of his actions.

'We got 30 years. But they let people who do sex crimes and things to little children out after a few years. Is that fair?'

His only possession now was a gold Rolex, which he habitually checked as if time had any meaning for him inside. His parting remark as the bell rang for the end of visiting time was perhaps the most revealing thing he had said during their brief time together. 'Promise you'll come back again.'

Enduring fascination

Three years later Callan interviewed Reggie Kray in Parkhurst, where he was serving life for the murder of George Cornell. The reporter described him as 'a man who exuded strength and hideous violence'. He was wearing a Lonsdale sweatshirt as a reminder to himself and his fellow inmates that he had been a boxer in his youth and might have been a contender. Prison had not diminished his physical or emotional stature. He was still an imposing presence who commanded other cons to stand when he walked by and he brought a smile to 'the sad, drained faces' of their wives on visiting day. Some of the women even reached out to touch him, as if this old lag might be persuaded to see their men through their long, lonely stretch inside; provided, of course, that they show him the required amount of reverence.

Callan conveyed the last words he had heard from Ronnie that day in Broadmoor: 'Tell him I'm happy.'

Then Callan asked Reggie if he regretted intimidating and terrorizing those who had crossed the Krays.

'Yeah, I do regret some of them things. And I do know I did frighten quite a lot of people. But I don't allow myself to live in the past.'

The reporter sensed a chance to coax a confession. How many people had he killed?

'Look, that's a libellous question,' Reggie answered with a glowering look and a steely tone in his voice. 'I'm in here for one murder.'

But then he must have thought better of it and admitted to stabbing Jack 'The Hat' McVitie to death, though he claimed it was self-defence.

'He boasted he was going to kill me with a shotgun.'

The law might not have seen it as justifiable homicide, but in Reggie's mind it amounted to the same thing. Kill or be killed, the law of the jungle. Referring to McVitie, Reggie added: 'He deserved it. Once, he stabbed someone in a club and came upstairs and wiped the knife on some women's dresses. Well, he wasn't such a nice guy, was he?'

Like the public enemies in Prohibition-era America, the Krays cultivated an image as charismatic 'lovable rogues', which seemed to attract celebrities and socialites. The twins were photographed in 1965 by fashion photographer David Bailey, who captured some of the iconic images of the Sixties. Like the Krays, Bailey was an East End boy-made-good and the Krays were similarly adopted as working-class heroes by chic society, although everyone knew how they made their money and enforced their stranglehold on the East End.

'He was a nice geezer,' Reggie remembered, referring to Bailey, who later remarked that 'real gangsters' didn't make the fatal mistake of courting publicity. But Reggie Kray wouldn't have listened to anyone's advice. He was too busy reminiscing about 'the good old days'. His words were full of nostalgia for the old East End, though they were certainly not sentimental.

Our enduring fascination with the Krays probably says more about the times we live in, and our own need to live vicariously through aggressively assertive personalities, than it does about the twins themselves. The one question Callan didn't ask them was if they thought it was all worth it. If they had known that they would spend the last 25 to 30 years inside – which was inevitable given their public contempt for the law and their bullish arrogance – would they still have chosen a life of crime? We can only guess what their answer must have been when the cell door closed and the lights went out each and every night.

Dominant personality types

The concept of the 'Right Man' or the 'Violent Man' was postulated by the Canadian writer A.E. Van Vogt (1912–2000) to identify and explain the behaviour of violent individuals (both male and female) whose outbursts of aggression often seem to be irrational and self-defeating. Although Van Vogt is better known as a prolific writer of science fiction, his psychological studies are of considerable value in understanding the thought processes of the violent criminal and those individuals who are incapable of controlling their anger and in so doing ultimately act against their own interests.

According to Van Vogt the 'Right Man' or Woman would 'cut off their nose to spite their face', as the saying goes. They would deliberately and knowingly immerse themselves in an increasing spiral of difficulty rather than admit the possibility that they might be wrong. Such people possess a highly inflated sense of self-importance and overreact to any perceived challenge to their beliefs or authority with vindictive indignation. This personality is typical of the dictator, the Mob boss, the dominant partner in an abusive relationship and the malignant matriarch or patriarch in a dysfunctional family, all of whom are tyrants in the eyes of their victims.

In a sense it is a form of insanity and it is all too common in personal and professional relationships where one partner seeks to control the other. The Right Man or Woman lives in their own fantasy and refuses to acknowledge the facts that conflict with their distorted worldview. An adoring wife, girlfriend or disciple who accepts everything they say without question only enforces their self-esteem and inflated sense of self-importance.

Van Vogt concluded that most violent men are failures and are beset by a deep-seated sense of inferiority, so that even a modicum of success will not compensate for their inner turmoil and fear of being made to confront their erroneous beliefs: 'If he suspects that his threats are not being taken seriously, he is capable of carrying them out, purely for the sake of appearances.'

Self-destructive impulses

Any violence he inflicts, he justifies to himself as appropriate punishment for disobedience or for being disrespectful. But it is he who is enslaved by his own uncontrollable emotions. As Colin Wilson observes, the violent individual 'is locked into a kind of vicious spiral, and he cannot escape until he has spent his fury'.

It is primarily, but not exclusively, males who submit to irrational violent impulses, partly because they have been conditioned to believe that it is socially acceptable for men to give vent to aggression. And when their dominance or primacy is questioned, many seek to redress what they see as the 'imbalance' by violent means.

In homicidal partnerships the controlling partner will gradually erode the other's freedom of movement, and contact with their family and friends, until they are entirely dependent on them. Like a charismatic cult leader, they will persuade their 'slave' that the outside world is a hostile place and that their only chance of survival is for the 'slave' to entrust his or her well-being and existence to their 'master', who of course knows best.

When the controlling partner is finally faced with the possibility of losing face and authority, or when the couple are threatened with capture and questioning, there is only one way out and that is self-destruction.

Wilson cites the example of a Californian mother, Elizabeth Duncan, who in 1958 hired two professional hitmen to kill her pregnant daughter-in-law because she did not think the young woman was a suitable wife for her son.

Duncan was insanely jealous of 30-year-old Olga Kupczyk, who had nursed her after a failed suicide attempt and then went on to marry her son, Frank. She even went to the lengths of posing as Olga and paying another man to pretend to be her son so that she could obtain an annulment.

The two young killers, Augustine Baldonado and Luis Moya, buried their victim alive in a shallow grave after beating her up and strangling her. When the assassins demanded their money, Duncan went to the police rather than pay them what she had promised because she was so outraged that they had the temerity to blackmail her. All three were tried, convicted and executed on the same day in August 1962.

Such highly dominant, psychotic personalities feel an overwhelming compulsion to act even when it is against their own interests. They simply can't control themselves.

Craving instant recognition

It is estimated that 5 per cent of the population in any given country are dominant personality types, but the majority of these eventually come to accept their role and their own particular level in society; what Wilson calls their 'lack of primacy'.

High dominance types are by nature impatient, so when the dominant individual witnesses the rise of 'ordinary' people to exalted status, conferring upon them celebrity, wealth and influence, they become resentful that their own 'uniqueness' has not been similarly recognized and acknowledged. Crime, and in particular violent crime, offers them the shortcut to the instant recognition that they crave and they assert themselves as forcibly as they can. As Wilson puts it: 'Self-pity and the sense of injustice make them vulnerable and unstable.'

And he goes on to make the crucial point that a person with a strong sense of purpose and a single-minded determination to achieve their goals is far less susceptible to the negative messages that the majority of his or her fellow beings are being bombarded with each and every day.

The aberrant personality craves continual stimulation and has been conditioned to expect only rejection, reproofs, criticism and disappointment. When they retaliate, they are punished for doing so and this begins the vicious circle in which they become trapped. As such, even the most intelligent criminal is unwilling to make the supreme effort of will to confront their own misconception of society as hostile, stupid and antagonistic. And he unconsciously blocks out everything that contradicts this view.

All of the cases cited in this book bear out the theory that aggressive individuals act in the belief that only violence will achieve their desires. They see themselves as victims of a cruel and indifferent world and respond instinctively out of all proportion to a perceived slight. Violence becomes a habitual reflex.

The Glasgow gangs

The Glasgow police are used to hearing accounts of 'alien abductions', but not all of them are the fantasies of drunks and drug addicts. They maintain an active case file on those abductions and many of them have a more rational explanation.

'Alien abductions' is a common term north of the border for the kidnapping of rival drug dealers, who are found wandering the streets in a daze, half-naked after allegedly being tortured by an enforcer believed to be working for the Daniel family, one of the most feared crime families in Glasgow, according to Scottish reporter Ron McKay. When the victims are found they claim they can't remember what happened, which gave some joker at Strathclyde police HQ the idea to name the file 'alien abductions'. The police know they are unlikely to put the perpetrators behind bars because the abductees are too scared to talk.

McKay claimed there's nothing amusing about the methods used by the Daniel gang and their hated rivals the Lyons when pursuing their 'business interests'. It's a brutal and bloody feud that has left many dead on both sides and more than a few innocent bystanders traumatized.

Their feud became public on 13 Friday 2010 when shoppers at a Glasgow Asda supermarket witnessed a 'hit' like a scene out of *The Godfather*. Three masked men strode up to a black Audi and shot the passenger in the back seat at point-blank range, killing him instantly. The two men in the front seat fled the scene, presumably by prior arrangement with the gunmen, or perhaps they were simply allowed to live so they could pass the message on to their employers. One of them then phoned a fellow gang member, who arrived at the scene before the police and recovered the dead man's mobile phone. Had it been found on the body, it might have provided information that could have embarrassed those members of the police who were suspected of taking bribes from the gang to impede the investigation. In fact, an officer was subsequently convicted of tipping off the alleged hitmen.

Gerbil

The victim was 29-year-old Kevin Carroll, known as 'Gerbil', and it is believed that he only escaped an earlier death by virtue of serving an 18-month stretch for the possession of high-velocity ammunition. He would have gone down for much longer had not a charge of possessing a sub-machine gun been dropped. It was third time unlucky for Carroll, who had survived two previous attempts on his life.

A trusted lieutenant who had chosen his side in the Strathclyde turf war when he was still in short trousers, Carroll was said to be the 'brains' behind the 'alien abductions' of the Lyons' dealers. He had been bullied at school by the Lyons brothers, Steven and Edward, and that had led him to befriend their enemy Robert Daniel and his buddy Francis 'Fraggle' Green, the man who is said to have recovered the phone from Gerbil's bullet-riddled body.

Gang feud

The rivalry went back a long way, to the 1990s, and originated with the distribution of drugs on their respective estates. The Lyons family, headed by Eddie Jnr and his brother David, owned Milton and the Daniel family, led by Jamie Daniel, dominated neighbouring Possil (a no-go area known locally as 'The Jungle'). Each enforced their claim with intimidation and deadly force. There were drive-by shootings, firebomb attacks, near-fatal hit and run 'accidents', knifings, beatings and accusations of witness intimidation, as well as allegations

The funeral of Kevin 'the Gerbil' Carroll in Glasgow: the dead man's girlfriend Kelly Green, wearing Gucci shades and a black coat, stands next to Debbi Mortimer, also in shades, partner of crime boss Jamie Daniel.

of widespread police corruption. Then it became personal when someone vandalized Garry Lyons' grave. The eight-year-old son of Eddie Jnr had died of leukaemia in 1991 and his father had sworn to rub out the supposed perpetrator, Kevin Carroll.

The rival families might have lived in uneasy peace had it not been for the fact that someone got greedy in the summer of 2001 and stole a large stash of the Daniels' cocaine and then sold it to the Lyons gang, who peddled it on the street as their own. Since then the tit-for-tat attacks have escalated and, though they each claim to live by the motto 'act for business not pleasure', it would appear that they derive considerable pleasure from inflicting damage and pain on the other gang.

It was small-time stuff at first, which the police could afford to ignore in the belief that the two gangs were preying on each other and no innocent bystanders would get caught in the crossfire, but in December 2006 the feud went public in a big way and the police could no longer stand on the sidelines.

MOT garage shooting

Applerow Motors in Lambhill, north Glasgow, a vehicle repair business owned by David Lyons, was the site of a fatal shooting by two masked men in long black coats. Walking casually on to the forecourt, they shot dead David's 21-year-old nephew Michael and wounded his 37-year-old cousin Steven and Robert 'Piggy' Pickett. Steven survived and soon after fled to Spain, where he is reported to have offered his services to an Irish drugs gang. Pickett, who was hit in the stomach, had played an active role in the Paisley drug wars and had been recently recruited by the Lyons family, along with two more Paisley hard men who were also lucky to leave the garage alive that day.

In case he didn't get the message, David Lyons received a demand for money following the shooting.

The boys owe me £25,000 and I want what's owed to me. It's for drugs. They all know what it's about. The money doesn't matter to me as it's got to be paid to the piper. I don't want the police, the boys, not even your wife, knowing about it. If you keep them out of this then all your lives can go back to normal as we are all losing money through this. If you have any tricks for my pickup man then all the deals are off. Remember to keep your mouth shut. No cameras, no surveillance, as the pickup man doesn't know nothing so he's no use to you. Drop off, 4pm Saturday. I'll draw you a map and X will mark the spot.

In the *Scottish Herald* and *Glasgow Evening Times*, McKay identified the two gunmen as Daniel family gang members James McDonald and Raymond Anderson. They were subsequently convicted and given record sentences of 35 years apiece, both of which were reduced to 30 on appeal. Pickett, who recovered from the shooting minus one healthy kidney, was sentenced to two years in prison for contempt of court after it was intimated that he had been paid off to perjure himself. When asked to identify the gunmen at their trial he stated that two other men should be in the dock.

High-rise crime

In July 2016 Jamie Daniel died after a long battle against cancer. He was 58 and his personal wealth was estimated to be £10 million. His place was taken by his son Steven, who for his own safety ran the family business from the Costa del Sol. Steven took his father's place by default, his brother Zander having been jailed for 13 years the previous year for heroin dealing.

The Scottish press published stories alleging that Jamie had begun his criminal career as a scrap metal dealer and was raised in a culture of crime and violence. He instilled the notion in his children that the world was a jungle and that the fittest and fiercest survive by grabbing whatever they can, by fair means or foul, and defending their feeding ground with violence. He had no reason to believe any different.

From the 1930s the city was a battleground for rival gangs who fought for control of the slum districts. Their weapon of choice was the cut-throat razor, which gave Glasgow the unenviable distinction of being known as 'Scar City'. The gangs boasted that their membership numbered in the hundreds and any excuse served for a brawl in the city centre, but the dividing factor was almost always religion. Catholic gangs preyed on Protestant gangs and took their fight to the football terraces whenever Rangers and Celtic were playing. In the 1960s and 1970s, the demolition of the slums served only to redistribute the rival gangs around the new estates: Drumchapel in the north, Castlemilk in the south and Easterhouse in the east of the city.

They had been planned as a high-rise paradise, but the lack of amenities and the failure to address the old rivalries meant that the enmity was simply transplanted to these urban wastelands, where the criminals could hide in the anonymous concrete tower blocks.

It was in this environment that the Lyons and Daniel families established their immensely profitable drug-dealing enterprises, which they protected with intimidation and brute force.

Even the old-school gangland characters noticed the change when they were released from prison. As heroin addiction became rife in the 1970s and 1980s, competition among the dealers and distributors intensified and so did the violence used to enforce their 'patches'.

The reduction in social services and employment cutbacks implemented during the Thatcher years probably did more for recruitment into the rival families than anything that had pushed their predecessors into crime. Glasgow became known as 'the murder capital' and the young teams, as they became known, outnumbered the gangs in London by ten to one.

Cast of characters

The cast of characters in this brutal drama and their diverse business and personal relationships would provide enough material for a long-running soap opera – a combination of *Brookside* and *The Sopranos* perhaps. It has already spawned a shelf's worth of books, the best of which is *Caught in the Crossfire* by investigative journalist Russell Findlay, whose efforts to disentangle the interwoven strands of the two criminal empires and expose their alleged links to corrupt local councillors and politicians nearly cost him his life in a vindictive acid attack.

Findlay described Jamie Daniel as a 'snarling, glowering presence' whose path to crime was dictated by the tragedies and demeaning poverty of his early life. As the head of the Daniel clan he instilled his family and their criminal associates with a 'burning hatred of the police'.

By contrast, 'cocky, small-time crook' Eddie Lyons Snr was reviled by his enemies for having snitched on the local thugs who cut him up on the Cadder housing estate in 1984, when he was 25. He and his family were hounded from their home and rehoused in Milton. They were then given police protection, which he is accused of having exploited ever since. After cultivating the support of local politicians, who backed his pitch to run the Chirnsyde Community Centre, aka 'Eddie's Club', he cast himself as a community leader. Again according to Ron McKay, the centre was thought to be the 'headquarters of his illegal drugs empire'. Eddie's enemies accused him of using the death of his eight-year-old son Garry from cancer in 1991 by raising funds which he is alleged to have misappropriated, including one million pounds of taxpayers' money.

Findlay describes him as 'the smiling, plausible puppet master who outwardly acted like the model citizen, concerned about tackling youth crime, while the boys peddled drugs and inflicted violence on both their enemies and innocents'.

The Daniel gang didn't even have to do their own dirty work. If any upright citizen protested at the treatment meted out to innocent local kids, they would be set upon by youths who wanted to impress Eddie Snr and be recruited into the gang.

But it was not just the hard men themselves and their acne-ridden hoodies who Glasgow residents believed were a stain on their city. Local politicians were also accused of abusing their powers to protect the family.

As Findlay wrote:

> For many long years the campaigners were arrogantly dismissed then smeared by those in power who inexplicably backed the perverse Chirnsyde regime.
>
> The campaigners' brave and determined battle revealed a murky nexus between criminals, police officers and politicians. Against the odds, they won their crusade and exposed how the cancerous Daniel vs Lyons feud seeped from the city's mean streets into the high echelons of the political elite . . .

Daniel gang: main players

A roll call of the Daniel crime clan in the *Scottish Sun* in May 2017 named and shamed the main players who were still active at the time.

Frances 'Fraggle' Green

Fraggle, Jamie's second son, was a close associate of murdered Daniel family enforcer Kevin 'Gerbil' Carroll. Carroll was not only a key member of the gang but had become part of the Daniel family through his involvement with Jamie's daughter, Kelly 'Bo' Green.

'Fraggle' was jailed for three and a half years in 2012 for sanctioning a vicious attack on an elderly woman, Susanne Simpson. His sidekick, Robert Daniel, got three years for his part in the attack.

Robert Daniel

Jamie's 42-year-old nephew, Robert Daniel, was ambushed by a gang of gunmen during a drive-by shooting in Stepps, a suburb of Glasgow, in March 2017. In 2005 he was jailed for eight years for his part in a £300,000 heroin bust.

Steven 'Bonzo' Daniel

Another of Jamie's nephews has 'business interests' in payday loan firm KeyCash, according to the *Sun*, and is also financially involved in car washes and cab firms.

Bonzo was cleared after a major probe into the Daniel crime clan, which saw Jamie's son Zander Sutherland imprisoned for drug dealing in June 2015. He is said to have close links to taxi tycoon Stevie 'Fat Controller' Malcolm and Edinburgh power-broker Mark Richardson.

The McGovernment

If Ron Mckay's damning reports on *Glasgow Live* were accurate, then the Lyons and Daniel families were not the only ones to recruit thugs from the unemployed, listless youths to be found hanging around every street corner. The McGovern family from Springburn became so powerful that they were referred to locally as the McGovernment.

The family consisted of five brothers, the eldest of whom, Tony, was shot dead by a former business partner in 2000, despite the fact that he was wearing a bulletproof vest. One of his younger brothers was shot in the face in a separate incident and survived. Tony's death left a vacancy at the head of the family, which was taken by Tony's brother-in-law, Russell Stirton. It was said that Stirton laundered his drugs money through his legitimate business, a filling station which sold the cheapest petrol in Britain.

Stirton was accused of having made his money by extortion, but after prosecutors had amassed sufficient evidence for his arrest, their witnesses mysteriously withdrew their statements and the case collapsed. Undeterred, the Crown chose a different approach, prosecuting Stirton under the Proceeds of Crime Act. This gave the authorities the power to prosecute criminals and recover their assets on the grounds that they were in all probability the proceeds of crime. As a result, Stirton was £5.6 million ($7m) the poorer and had three houses repossessed, while the public were faced with a legal aid bill for £250,000 ($316,000). In October 2015, he was the beneficiary of a further £932,273 ($1.1m) in legal aid to contest the seizure of his assets.

Confiscating the proceeds of crime

The Proceeds of Crime Act was also used to confiscate the assets of a less prominent member of the Daniel family – Annette, sister of Jamie. She and Jean McGovern were accused of operating a highly lucrative shoplifting ring which targeted Knightsbridge stores such as Harrods. Their partnership was said to employ hundreds of light-fingered individuals who have taken shoplifting to a new level, netting their female bosses millions every year. In a single raid in May 2012, which was as meticulously planned as any jewel heist, they were believed to have acquired £24,000 ($30,000) of designer dresses from Harrods.

And though Annette has a string of convictions for shoplifting, she has only had to repay a fraction of her ill-gotten gains, a mere £25,000 ($31.000) on one occasion, and has spent no longer than 18 months in prison. It was evident from her protests at one memorable court appearance that she regards thieving from legitimate businesses as a career choice and any attempt to prevent her from helping herself as unfair. As she was led from the dock to begin her sentence she yelled: 'This is against my human rights, so it is.'

McMafia

In January 2017 there was an attempted hit on a Lyons associate, Ross Monaghan, as he dropped his daughter off at school. He survived with gunshot wounds to the shoulder and hand, but bringing the feud home to the families was considered off-limits and there were reprisals including vicious machete attacks, one of which was said to have left Steven 'Bonzo' Daniel disfigured for life.

The feud had got out of control and even the police had to admit they could do with some outside help. It is believed someone in authority approached MI5, the British intelligence agency, and the National Crime Agency, to intervene. They came up with an ingenious solution – approach a former Glasgow gang boss with some form of deal regarding immunity from prosecution and appeal to his ego by asking him to broker a pact between the warring parties.

An unnamed source told the Scottish *Daily Record*:

The expat criminal was in London on business when he was approached by either the security services or the NCA. He was asked to use his influence by relaying the message to both sides that the bloodshed in Scotland had to end. Unfortunately, it seems not to have had the desired effect. There has been so much violence that neither side seems willing to back down. The approach has also instilled a sense of paranoia in both camps about who can be trusted and who is looking at them.

It is not the first time the security services and the police have cooperated to crack down on Britain's organized crime families. They had success with smashing drug gangs in London and Manchester, including the notorious Adams family (see page 213).

Turf war behind bars

Meanwhile, the police immobilized dozens of vehicles thought to be used by both families in their criminal activities, using DVLA number-plate recognition. By clamping the untaxed and uninsured cars, repossessing those which had unpaid loans and impounding others which had been stolen, the police hoped to hamper the gang's 'business', specifically the distribution of drugs. In one car they seized a large quantity of heroin and other vehicles may provide the police with crucial DNA that could identify those involved in fatal shootings and other vicious attacks.

Detective Superintendent Kenny Graham told the press:

Our aim is to disrupt the day-to-day activities of organised crime groups and their families in their own backyards.

The Daily Record, *8.12.2006: The execution of Michael Lyons took place in a vehicle repair business owned by crime family member David Lyons after two armed men showed up in masks and long black coats.*

We're also working with the HMRC, DVLA and DWP to target their legitimate businesses, assets, possessions and unexplained wealth. In this case, we've been targeting their cars, many of which are high-value and high-performance. We use traditional policing methods but also look into their lifestyles. We look into their backgrounds. We ask what type of businesses they're involved in and we target that.

But the police are not the only ones the criminals have to worry about. The turf war is continued behind bars so that even in jail the gang members have to watch their backs.

In February 2018, Daniel associate Steven Wilkinson was beaten up in the exercise yard of Glasgow's Barlinnie prison. Wilkinson had been sentenced to six years for possessing a Skorpion sub-machine pistol, ammunition and a silencer, which the prosecution argued was going to be used to assassinate a leading member of the Lyons family.

The Skorpion is a favoured weapon of terrorist groups and the Scottish crime families are known to have paid up to £15,000 for one. Most worrying is the suspicion that the feuding families obtained theirs from a rogue British Army unit who have been selling weapons, ammunition and explosives to Glasgow's underworld.

The Adams family

The criminal activities of the Adams family of north London make their Scottish counterparts look like small-time hoods by comparison.

The three Adams brothers, Terry, Patrick and Tommy, were said to head one of the most powerful criminal syndicates in the UK and to have links to international drug cartels in Latin America. Their illicit fortune is estimated at over £200 million ($253m), though Terry pleaded poverty at an appeal hearing in December 2017, in a vain attempt to avoid repaying a court order for £720,000 ($910,000), which amounted to a fraction of his 'criminal earnings'. The police once described the brothers as 'worse than the Krays', although their formidable reputation apparently led to them being credited with crimes that other gangs had committed.

During their 30-year reign the A-team, as they were commonly known, were believed to have been behind at least 25 murders, including that of their own financial adviser, Solly Nahome, who was shot by a motorbike rider in a hit that bore the hallmarks of an Adams-sanctioned assassination. They were also believed to have been responsible for the botched shooting of 'Mad' Frankie Fraser in 1991, a former cohort of south London gangsters Charlie and Eddie Richardson. When asked who shot him, Fraser answered: 'If you play by the sword, you've got to expect the sword as well.'

Other killings were attributed to the Adams family, but none of the brothers were prosecuted as they rarely got their own hands dirty. They were eventually caught and convicted after Tommy went solo in a drugs venture that had not been approved by his brothers.

Teflon Terry

Terry Adams was the oldest of 11 children born to Irish-Catholic parents who lived in a cramped north London council flat. He began making a name for himself by running an extortion racket, squeezing small change from market stall holders, shopkeepers and pub owners in his own borough of Clerkenwell, London, in the 1980s, but he soon graduated to drug dealing, security fraud, white-collar crime and gold bullion heists. Tommy was charged with fencing gold from the £28 million Brink's-Mat bullion robbery at Heathrow airport in 1983, but left court a free man.

Terry and Patrick Adams were suspected of involvement in other armed robberies, but no one could make the charges on 'Teflon' Terry stick. Patrick wasn't so lucky and was sent down for seven years in the 1970s. He was again jailed for nine years in December 2016, for shooting one of his former partners, Paul Tiernan.

The British Godfather

When Tommy went inside for seven and a half years for drug trafficking, Terry filled his shoes and was accused of making a fortune supplying drugs to the rave generation. He ran the family business as if it was a legitimate concern and earned himself the title 'The British Godfather', allegedly enforcing his sovereignty with kneecapping and other brutal acts of intimidation.

It was further alleged that the Adams family sanctioned the liquidation of their own hitman and their chief bookkeeper to preserve the family secrets.

Terry's personal share of their estimated £100 million ($126m) fortune gave him the readies to buy £1.5 million ($1.9m) house in leafy Mill Hill, north London without having to ask for a mortgage. The five-bedroom house boasts four bathrooms and a private gym. It was refurbished at a cost of £222,000 ($281,000) and contains £500,000 ($633,000) worth of antiques and art, including a Henry Moore etching and several priceless lino cuts by Picasso. It could belong to any nouveau riche lottery winner except for two tell-tale signs – the £12,000 ($15,000) security system with video intercoms and spike-topped electric gates and the screen print of Al Pacino hanging over the wall-mounted plasma TV in the living room. It was Terry's main home, although he also owns properties abroad and a luxury yacht.

Terry Adams was alleged to have made a fortune supplying drugs to the rave generation.

He evidently saw himself as a Pacino figure and was known for his expensive taste in clothes – ruffled shirts and velvet suits – which prompted one commentator to describe him as a cross between nightclub owner Peter Stringfellow and Liberace. He was also feared for his volatile temper.

At his own restaurant, Beluga, in North Finchley, he could be seen to demonstrate his displeasure when one of his enforcers spoke out of turn. According to a witness quoted in the *Daily Mail* in 2009:

> Terry put down his knife and fork slowly. Then he whacked the guy full in the face. We heard his nose crack. There was blood all over him. Then Terry picked up his knife and fork and carried on eating. We all did the same. So did the guy with the smashed nose.

But money couldn't buy him everything he wished for. When Tottenham Hotspur football club was up for sale, he couldn't bid for it because it was said that his offer would not be accepted as it was considered tainted money. There were no objections, however, to his takeover of a string of Soho sex shops.

Corrupt police officers

By investing the proceeds in the family business they were able to expand into other profitable illegal enterprises and recruit more members of their extended family as well as trusted outsiders. At one point it is believed that they allowed other London gangs to use their name to intimidate those who owed them money.

To protect their interests the Adams family are alleged to have procured the services of corrupt Metropolitan police officers and at least one Conservative MP, as well as Jamaican Yardie gangs, who they employed to silence informers and discourage rival gangs from trespassing on their territory. A classified report into police corruption concluded that officers had sabotaged an investigation into the 1995 murder of drug dealer Michael Olymbious, which the brothers were suspected of having ordered. A crucial eyewitness statement was subsequently found in a flat above a club owned by Terry Adams.

So pervasive was the Adams family's alleged influence on the British judicial system, that it was only with the assistance of MI5 that 62-year-old Terry was finally convicted and the extent of the brothers' illicit activities became public. At Terry Adams' trial the prosecution stated:

> It is suggested that Terry Adams was one of the country's most feared and revered organized criminals.
>
> He comes with a pedigree, as one of a family whose name had a currency all of its own in the underworld.
>
> A hallmark of his career was the ability to keep his evidential distance from any of the violence and other crime from which he undoubtedly profited.

After all their meticulous planning and Terry Adams' strenuous efforts to distance himself from the day-to-day dealings of his criminal empire, the gang were finally undone by carelessness on the part of his brother Tommy, who foolishly hired a taxi firm to collect their debts.

Police and the security services bugged a café in central London where 59-year-old Tommy met with his associates and by eavesdropping on their conversations they were able to put surveillance teams on the couriers who were sent to collect tens of thousands of pounds in cash owed to Tommy for the sale of drugs.

The press revealed that the bugged recordings contained numerous references to the punishments he had ordered to be meted out to former rivals and double-crossing associates.

In one he was alleged to have said: 'When I hit someone with something I do them damage. And I went to the geezer and I went crack. On my baby's life, Dan, his kneecap come right out there . . . all white, Dan, all bone . . . '

The high cost of bringing criminals to court

In November 2017, after an investigation which lasted two years and cost the taxpayer £50 million, Tommy Adams was convicted on two counts of conspiracy to conceal and transport criminal property and was sentenced to seven years. MI5 also bugged Terry Adams' home, which provided significant leads that led to his arrest and conviction on charges of money laundering.

The brothers had kept 'thousands' of handwritten notes which detectives found while investigating one of the 25 gangland murders they suspected were linked to the family. They mentioned a 'shadow account' and referred to a ledger which was later recovered and decoded.

Tommy's carelessness also brought down several of his best 'customers', who were caught in the operation bringing pay-offs from Manchester to London to settle their debts for drugs and other services. Tommy's 32-year-old son Shaun was also convicted for his part in the crimes, though his 35-year-old daughter Terri was freed after denying 'fraud by false representation' and was able to enjoy the fruits of her father's activities, including a £32,000 ($40,000) car he had given her as a present.

In sentencing the brothers the judge remarked that 'the evidence demonstrated significant planning, contrivance and subterfuge', though the prosecution added that the charges only highlighted one aspect of the gang's criminal activities. The cash seized from the couriers and from an address in London was only a small part of the income from the family's drugs operation according to the prosecution, who told the jury that there had been many such runs.

Entrepreneurs

In the wake of the successful prosecution of Terry and Tommy, the fourth and youngest of the Adams brothers, 52-year-old Michael, was jailed in June 2018 for defrauding the taxman of around half a million pounds in unpaid tax over a period of eight years by falsely declaring his income. Other members of the Adams family were not accused of being involved in the four brothers' criminal activities.

Gangland expert Wensley Clarkson said:

> The Adamses are probably the last of the old-school British crime families.
>
> They're a bit like the Sopranos – they made their money and then sent their children to private schools, bought art, invested in legal businesses. Terry, in particular, is very bright. In another era, another world, he could have been head of a major international corporation, and that's how these people see themselves, in a way.

Young pretenders

The jailing of Terry and the seizure of a significant amount of the Adams family's assets created the opportunity for a new generation of volatile young 'wannabe' criminals eager to move in on their territory.

These 'low level' teenage criminals earning £100 ($125) a day dealing drugs on the capital's street corners are impatient to make a name for themselves, which has led to a spate of vicious and seemingly random knife attacks. The fatal stabbing of 16-year-old Ben Kinsella in 2008, shortly after Terry Adams was jailed for money laundering, led to widespread rumours that the family were 'unhappy' about the killing on their turf and had sent a message to their associates to avenge his death. Although the family had no relationship with the victim and their business interests were not under threat, they had to be seen to be controlling their 'manor', even from inside prison.

As a police source told the *Guardian* newspaper: 'They may have a low profile these days, but there remains a powerful mythology surrounding the Adamses.'

Shortly after the word was out, the young ringleader of the gang who killed Kinsella gave himself up to the police.

Chapter Six:
The Mafia

Evil is unspectacular and always human and shares our
bed and eats at our own table.

W.H. Auden (1907–73), English-American poet

Breaking the code

In April 2011 a New York court witnessed an unprecedented appearance by a Mafia 'Godfather', who took the stand to testify against his own 'family' and in doing so broke the sacred code of silence known to the Mob as '*omertà*'.

Sixty-eight-year-old Joseph C. Massino, known as 'the last Don', admitted to sanctioning the murders of numerous rivals and having the power to 'make and break' senior members of one of the five most powerful organized crime 'families' in the city, the Bonanno family. Massino held the packed federal district court's attention for almost five hours as he explained the intricate structure of his organization, its illegal business interests and the killings which had enforced its stranglehold on unions and legitimate businesses in New York for decades.

The former restaurant owner flavoured his confession with culinary metaphors to the amusement of the jury and the public gallery, which suggested that he wished to distance himself from the brutal nature of the beatings and 'hits' he had ordered.

'If you need somebody to kill somebody, you need workers,' he said. 'It takes all kinds of meat to make a good sauce.'

Massino himself was not on trial. He was merely a key witness

Joseph Massino with Gene Gotti, brother of John, outside Brooklyn Federal Court, 1986.

in the prosecution of his predecessor, Vincent Basciano, who was accused of ordering the murder of associate Randolph Pizzolo in 2004, but he was the centre of rapt attention that day and he clearly revelled in it.

He recounted his career in crime, which began with petty theft at the tender age of 12, and his graduation to becoming a key and indispensable member of the Bonanno family in the 1960s. When he eventually became head of the organization in 1991, he had hundreds of 'soldiers' and associates under his direct command and was continually having to appease the various factions. As such, he portrayed himself as a shrewd strategist and a wise arbitrator of internal disputes, as well as a man who had outfoxed both his gangland rivals and the forces of the federal government. He had devised a number of intricate codes so his lieutenants could talk freely without incriminating themselves and he ordered the closure of clubs which could be bugged by the FBI. If the bureau wanted to tail a member or associate of the Bonanno family, he reasoned, they would have to put at least one man on each suspect, which would stretch their resources and make surveillance practically impossible.

He had seen too many movies to make the mistake of discussing 'family business' in a potentially compromised location. 'You never talk in a club, you never talk in a car, you never talk on a cellphone, you never talk on a phone, you never talk in your house,' he told the prosecutor. The safest place to hold a meeting was on the street, in the open or in a walk-in cold storage facility located at one of his catering premises.

But faced with the death penalty for orchestrating eight murders, he had taken the crucial decision to turn state's evidence against members of the Mob and now faced life in prison rather than certain death at the hands of his own executioners.

Down but not out

The case came to court at a time when the law enforcement authorities were claiming they had broken the back of the five families after making a significant number of arrests of key players. But the Mafia had taken hits before and survived. Over the past decade four of the rival families had suffered from defections, while Massino had maintained an iron grip on his people following the damning public revelations made by the undercover FBI agent 'Donnie Brasco' in the 1980s. (Agent Joseph D. Pistone, aka 'Donnie Brasco', spent six years posing as a member of the Bonanno family.) The Genovese family then closed ranks to protect itself from penetration by possible future bureau 'plants'.

On this occasion the damage done to the Mob by Massino's 'treachery' was offset by the Bush administration's impulsive face-saving decision to divert resources away from fighting organized crime to battling terrorism and white-collar crime, which the White House saw as a priority. The authorities were beginning to believe that they had critically weakened three of the five families, thanks to informants, defectors and the RICO laws (Racketeer Influenced and Corrupt Organizations Act of 1970), which held Mafia bosses personally responsible for criminal acts carried out by their subordinates. But the diversion of resources has allowed the New York families to regenerate themselves and recapture lost ground and influence.

The rackets

The Mafia initially made their fortunes through racketeering, which meant extortion, loan sharking, money laundering, prostitution, pornography, fraud, kidnapping, illegal gambling and bootlegging, but they soon graduated to muscling in on the labour unions, taking a hefty cut of membership fees. More recently, they have turned to the wholesale distribution of hard drugs to street corner dealers.

Extortion and protection rackets brought comparatively small but regular payments to 'resolve' or avert disrupting labour strikes and loan sharking raked in substantial amounts from the semi-legal lending of money at outrageously high interest rates, with threats of violence for late or non-payment.

Virtually every legitimate business in America made backdoor payments to organized crime families in order to operate unhindered by 'accidents', arson attacks and trade-crippling union disputes. Many still grudgingly accept that a percentage of their stock will have to be written off to 'water damage' and other deductible losses so it can be given as 'gifts' to organized crime cartels.

The real Sopranos

In New York, the five families still control and profit from practically every legitimate money-making concern in the city and protect their own interests with bribes to corrupt politicians and law enforcement officials. Although each of the five families has been disrupted by internal rifts and interfactional violence, they haven't allowed these to interrupt the ceaseless flow of money into the family firms.

Genovese

The Genovese family are the aristocracy of the New York underworld, with roots dating back to the Prohibition era. In 1931 Charles 'Lucky' Luciano knocked a few heads together to bring the protracted and bloody war between the Masseria gang and the Sicilian Castellammare del Golfo gang to an end and convinced the two factions to form an alliance. Lucky then had Masseria murdered so that his adversary

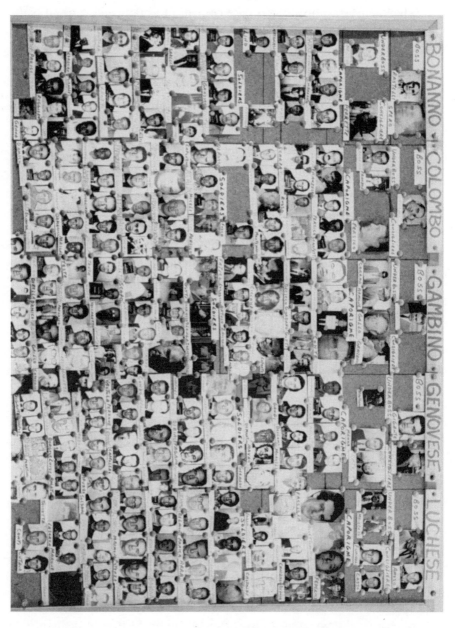

A bulletin board compiled by the NYPD, 1988, showing the five big organized crime families.

Salvatore Maranzano could take control of organized crime in New York. Maranzano restructured the numerous Italian-American gangs into five 'families' and gave each of them a slice of the city, to avoid squabbles over territory. He also rewarded Lucky by appointing him head of the newly formed Morello/Masseria 'family'. But Lucky was ambitious and had Maranzano 'rubbed out' five months later, leaving himself in overall control of organized crime in the city.

In anticipation of future conflicts of interest and disagreements Luciano established a governing body composed of representatives from each of the five families, to act as arbitrators in disputes. That commission still exists today and serves to keep the five families from killing each other off completely.

The Genovese name was attributed to the Luciano gang after Vito Genovese took over from Luciano in 1957. Although based in New York, like the other four families, the Genovese family extended their activities throughout the United States and beyond, but they are said to have lost considerable clout and credibility after the death of their last figurehead, Vincent Gigante, in 2005. Gigante was known as 'the Oddfather' because he wandered the streets of New York in a shower robe in a vain attempt to persuade the FBI that he was insane and therefore unfit to stand trial.

Gambino

The Gambino crime family is believed to operate on both the East and West coasts and was arguably the most powerful Mafia family in America until 1992. That year the second most senior member, Sammy Gravano, turned state's evidence against his boss, John Gotti, and the family powerbase suffered irreparable damage from which it never recovered.

The Oddfather: in his trademark bathrobe, Vincent 'Chin' Gigante walks the streets of New York City arm in arm with his brother, Father Louis Gigante, a Catholic priest.

In the 1950s, the then head of the Gambino family, Albert Anastasia, founded Murder Incorporated, an independent agency which provided hitmen for a price and the promise that the killings would not be traced back to the bosses who had hired them.

After Anastasia was murdered by his own men in 1957, his place was taken by Carlo Gambino, who kept out of the public eye and subsequently avoided spending a single day in jail during the 20 years he headed the family business. When Gambino died in 1976, he was succeeded by his brother-in-law, Paul Castellano, who ran the organization along semi-legitimate lines, which infuriated the more violent-minded members who felt they should be out on the streets squeezing money with menaces and not sitting behind desks filling out paperwork. Eventually, in 1985, they turned on Castellano and he was murdered with the approval of his own family, who installed John Gotti as the Boss of Bosses. When Gotti was imprisoned, his son

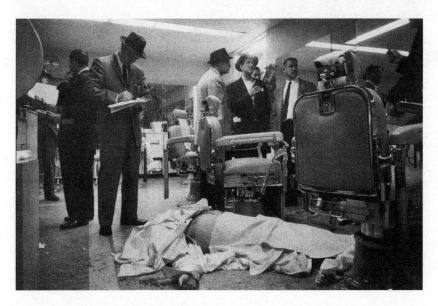

Detectives comb the barbershop at the Park Sheraton Hotel, New York for clues after Albert Anastasia was shot dead there in 1957.

John Gotti Jnr took his place, keeping control and the lion's share of the profits in the family.

Lucchese

Tommy 'Three-Fingers' Lucchese, so called because of an industrial accident which deprived him of his right thumb and forefinger, became boss of the downtown crime family in 1951 and his heirs kept control of the business for the next 50 years.

The Luccheses had their fingers in many lucrative pies including haulage, clothing, construction, catering and the unions, as well as controlling freight at the three New York airports. But in the late 1980s internal rifts threatened to destroy the family. Two underbosses, Vittorio 'Vic' Amuso and Anthony Casso, initiated one of the most violent periods in the history of organized crime, ordering hits on rival families and taking out those they distrusted within their own ranks. The resulting bloodbath led to a top Casso aide spilling his guts to the FBI, who were then able to round up all the major players in the Lucchese family. Casso himself cooperated in the prosecution of his former associates, leaving a crippled organization to be run by Amuso from his prison cell.

The Lucchese family are said to have been the inspiration for the fictitious Mafia family portrayed in the TV series *The Sopranos*, while the confessions of former Lucchese associate Henry Hill provided the basis for the Martin Scorsese movie *Goodfellas*.

Colombo

The Colombo crime family is actually run by the Persico family whose senior member, Carmine 'The Snake' Persico, has been pulling the strings since he took control in the 1970s. Quite a feat considering he has been in jail for the greater part of his tenure. However, in

Dapper John Gotti with Salvatore 'the Bull' Gravano (right) arriving for the funeral of bodyguard Shorty Mascuzzio who was killed in a West side disco after he pistol-whipped the owner.

comparison to the other four families the Colombo family is regarded as the least powerful, having been weakened by three major internal power struggles since the 1960s, when Joseph Colombo took the reins and attempted to heal the rifts within his organization.

According to Mafia tradition, a jailed boss can retain his status as Don if he wishes to remain in control and siphon off his share of the profits, but only if he has a trusted lieutenant on the outside to enforce his orders. Carmine had his elder brother Alphonse to ensure his edicts were carried out, but Alphonse jumped bail on loan-sharking charges a year later. The subsequent conviction of Carmine's son Michael appears to signal the end of the Persico era.

Carmine's failure to resolve the infighting, which saw 48 members and associates imprisoned and a dozen more turn informant, prompted the Commission to consider dissolving the family to avoid further embarrassment. But in the end they held back their decision to see if the Colombo leadership could put its own house in order.

Bonanno

The Bonanno family, named after founder Joseph 'Joe Bananas' Bonanno, at 26 the youngest Mafia 'Godfather', was disavowed by the Commission due to its participation in heroin dealing, which was prohibited by the governing body. Further humiliation came with the discovery that an FBI undercover agent had infiltrated their ranks and disclosed incriminating evidence accumulated over a period of six years. However, the family's dismissal from the Commission proved to be a lucky break when the Mafia's governing body found itself on trial in the 1980s. The Bonannos were able to exploit the temporary power vacuum, though they received a potentially fatal blow when boss Joseph Massino broke cover to confess all in open court in April 2011 (see beginning of chapter).

The Bonannos had been the most stable and impenetrable of the five families in the early days, thanks to their membership being restricted to Sicilians from Bonanno's home town, Castellammare del Golfo. The Bonannos were further strengthened by their business and personal alliance with the Profaci family, which came with the marriage of Bonanno's son Salvatore to Joe Profaci's niece Rosalie in 1956. But after the death of Joe Profaci six years later, the Lucchese and Gambino families saw their chance and formed an alliance to put the squeeze on the Bonanno empire.

The family was under further threat from within when a civil war broke out between rival factions, which the press dubbed 'the banana split'. A Brooklyn 'summit meeting' saw heated exchanges which quickly exploded into a gun battle, though no one was killed. The opposing sides then took their war on to the streets and even the intervention of the Commission failed to bring them to their senses. It was only when Joseph Bonanno took early 'retirement' that an uneasy truce was arranged.

But the Bonannos continued to be a stone in the shoe of the other families, who resented the fortune they made from dealing in heroin. Despite this, the family weathered the periodic rifts by recruiting the sons of 'made men' to keep it all in the family and insisting that 'soldiers' proved their loyalty by serving under a made man for eight years before they could apply to become 'made men' themselves.

The Bonanno family became the most powerful of the five families during the 1990s, but in 2004 capo Joseph Massino became the first Mafia 'Godfather' to betray his family when faced with the death penalty. He had sanctioned the hit on caporegime (lieutenant or head of a 'crew' of soldiers) Dominick Napolitano, who had allowed his family to be infiltrated by FBI agent Joseph Pistone.

Joe Bonanno stops to talk to UPI reporter Robert Evans on the steps of the federal courthouse as he surrenders himself to the authorities after a worldwide manhunt lasting 19 months. It began when he was reportedly kidnapped at gunpoint before a scheduled appearance in front of a rackets grand jury.

The Dons must have been spinning in their graves when their heir turned FBI informant and broke the sacred oath of *omertà*.

Wiseguys

As some wit once remarked, Mafia bosses like to think they are smart, but they never seem to learn from their mistakes. Neither do they ever come to realize the true cost of making their reputations, which is always at someone else's expense.

Take Carmine Persico, for example. The notoriously hot-tempered head of the Colombo crime family has spent 40 years of his life in prison knowing that his sons, brothers and many other male relatives are also wasting their lives away in captivity. No doubt they console themselves by reliving memories of the day they were feted like princes in their neighbourhood, walking tall through the city streets in sharp suits, with gold Rolexes on their wrists and diamond rings on their fingers, and having everyone acknowledge their supremacy: the biggest, meanest beasts in the jungle. But every night they are led back to their cells and every morning they wake up in the same cell knowing they are no longer free to walk those same streets.

Those very people who appeared to fear and 'respect' them are doubtless breathing easier, knowing they won't be seeing Carmine and his kind for a very long time – if ever. The Colombo family are estimated to be worth a billion dollars, which makes Carmine one of the wealthiest 'wiseguys' in Mafia history, but he can't spend it. He won't be tipping the waiters big in chic nightclubs, or ordering any more thousand-dollar suits.

As his biographers Frank DiMatteo and crime writer Michael Benson point out in *Carmine Persico and His Murderous Mafia Family*, the Mafia life is 'a lie'. DiMatteo, himself a jailed Mafia 'survivor', confesses that for 45 years he had 'blinders on' and came to the sobering conclusion that he had lived 'a lie'.

> My father was with the Gallo brothers from the time I was a baby, and I was raised to believe that the Gallo crew was my family. I called many of those guys 'uncle'. They moulded me into an up-and-coming hood, led me to believe that we were family – that we had to stick together. They taught me that everyone outside the family was wrong, bad, the enemy.

But he came to realize – and to see for himself – that 'you get stabbed in the back when you're not needed anymore'.

He had been told that Carmine had been like a brother to Larry Gallo and that Carmine had turned on his 'brother' and attempted to kill him when the opportunity arose to 'climb the ladder'. At the time Carmine had been damned for doing so, but now DiMatteo could see that Carmine was no different than his predecessors in his self-serving determination to rise to the top of the heap on the bodies of others. He was only following in the footsteps of Joe 'the Boss' Masseria (who murdered his superior Salvatore D'Aquila); Salvatore Maranzano (who had iced his boss Alfred Manfredi); Albert Anastasia (who liquidated Vincent Mangano); Carlo Gambino (who in turn dispatched Anastasia); or John Gotti (for ordering the elimination of Paul Castellano). By comparison with those men, Lucky Luciano was merciful – he 'allowed' Frank Scalice to step aside and walk away from that life.

DiMatteo put his finger on it when he wrote:

> Carmine Persico's life is best measured by what he destroyed, the pain and death and suffering he left in

his wake . . . He destroyed his own blood family. His older brother died in prison, his younger brother spent twenty-two years behind bars, both he and his eldest son will likely die in prison . . . Family members that remain free are stigmatized by their name . . .

He concludes that Carmine helped to destroy his own crime family, the Colombos, by insisting that the Persicos retain control by right of blood, rather than concede power to those who were considered to have earned the right to lead – even when he and his brood were behind bars and their influence was weakened as a result.

'Little Al' breaks the sacred oath of silence

Alfonso D'Arco, acting boss of the Lucchese crime family, knew he was only moments away from death. He had been invited to what he had been told was a regular business meeting with his associates in a Manhattan hotel room – men he had known for years and had come to trust, men who had taken the same oath of loyalty as he had – but now he knew they had lured him into a fatal trap.

He had heard the rumours on the streets of Little Italy that summer, the summer of 1991, that he was no longer to be trusted, that he had turned informer – which was not true – but once a made man was suspected of treason there was no hope of talking his way out of it. The Lucchese family had become paranoid, obsessed with betrayal, and saw treachery round every corner. D'Arco had killed other men on his superiors' say so, though he personally doubted they deserved it. But you don't question orders, if you want to stay vertical. Now he sensed that he was next.

For their own safety, former friends had been keeping their distance, or had been unavailable when he called. Some had suddenly found themselves unexpectedly busy when he'd asked for a meeting to talk things through. But it was only when he noticed a concealed weapon in the waistband of one of the men in that hotel room that he instinctively knew they had only called the meeting to entrap him.

What he heard next made him determined to bring them all down, if he could only leave the room alive. An associate from another New York family was telling the others how he would ensure no 'made man' ever turned informer again: he would liquidate the man's entire family. 'Little Al' felt a chill. He had to save his own family – whatever the cost – so he found some excuse and left the room, before anyone had a chance to stop him.

A few nights later he called an FBI agent and asked for a meeting. At the time, he was the highest-ranking member of the Mafia to turn informer, but he had no second thoughts about telling all he knew. There was no longer any honour in being a made man, not when they were prepared to kill the families of those they only suspected of betraying them. His former masters and the 'soldiers' who served them were no longer criminals, they were evil. He was convinced of that.

He subsequently appeared as a key witness in more than a dozen high-profile Mafia-related trials, resisting the most aggressive cross-examination and demonstrating a phenomenal memory for dates, names and details that earned him the respect of his FBI handlers, if not the defence.

Over the next ten years, his testimony led to the conviction of 50 high-ranking members of the Mafia, among them the bosses of four of the five New York families. Other defendants accepted plea bargains rather than take their chances with juries who would hear the shocking details of their crimes from one of their own.

According to his biographers, Jerry Capeci and Tom Robbins, 'Little Al' was able to provide the names of 26 Mob factions active in Sicily and also where their stateside representatives could be found. He detailed the illegal business interests of the families who had skimmed money from government construction projects and named the family which had infiltrated the trade unions. At the same time, he also cleared up a couple of dozen cold case files.

He was even able to offer a chronological history of the Mafia as he had been taught it by his mentors back in the late 1940s and early 1950s, such as the unknown alliance between automobile manufacturer

Henry Ford and the Mob. They were given a valuable contract to transport vehicles hot off the conveyor belt in the New Jersey plant to dealerships, in exchange for breaking the unions, a contract which the federal agents were subsequently able to verify.

Drugs and the Dons – the Mafia myth

Mafia movies have propagated one of the more persistent myths about La Cosa Nostra ('this thing of ours') and that is that 'men of honour', as they like to call themselves, do not deal in hard drugs. Even under oath on the witness stand in a federal court, Mob bosses such as Salvatore Gravano ('Sammy the Bull') have testified that they have a 'policy' against dealing in narcotics.

But as far back as the 'Roaring Twenties', men such as Lucky Luciano were raking in fortunes from importing and distributing cocaine. And in 1959 Vito Genovese, head of one of the five New York crime 'families', was sentenced for distributing drugs. Although several bosses had made their opposition to drug distribution known, it was primarily to protect their own interests, as the federal government was funnelling its considerable resources into its well-publicized 'war on drugs'.

Even so, in the 1970s and 1980s the Mafia couldn't keep their fingers out of such a lucrative business and ran a drug distribution ring on the East Coast using pizzerias as a front. Over a five-year period, from 1979–84, 1,650 lbs (748 kg) of heroin was smuggled into the United States and distributed to dealers, netting the Bonanno family and their partners an estimated $1.6 million (worth $4m/£3.16m now).

But federal law enforcement officers had the Bonannos under surveillance and after a four-year investigation they finally had enough evidence to prosecute them. The resulting trial lasted almost three years and saw 19 defendants arraigned on drugs charges, 17 of whom were convicted and imprisoned at a cost to the American taxpayer of $50 million (around $120m/£95m today).

The two major defendants, Gaetano Badalamenti, a former head of the Sicilian Mafia and Salvatore Catalano, a boss of the Bonanno family, were sentenced to 45 years apiece. Catalano served 29 years before being released, but Badalamenti died in jail. Two more defendants struck a plea bargain, a third was acquitted, another pleaded guilty while recovering from a failed attempt on his life and a fifth failed to appear because he had been murdered and his body dumped in a garbage bin.

Further arrests were made outside the States, revealing a link between the Bonanno family, the Sicilian Mafia and organized crime factions in Europe and South America. Cocaine was supplied by the South Americans, connections in Turkey provided morphine and the Sicilians processed the heroin. The financial network that was set up to siphon the money was so convoluted that even the prosecutors and defence attorneys needed diagrams to make sense of it all.

The prosecution case was further hampered by the fact that many of the defendants were Sicilian and claimed not to be able to speak English. When they talked among themselves even the translators were unable to decipher the essential details because they spoke in code. The complexity and protracted nature of the proceedings formed the basis of a string of appeals which were eventually denied, but the case backfired on the government. Instead of being seen to have been tough on organized crime they looked as if they couldn't organize the proverbial celebration in a pizzeria.

The threat of violence was ever present, with accusations of witness intimidation, threats to the life of the judge and jury tampering, all of which seemed far more than rumour-mongering when one of the defendants, pizzeria owner Gaetano Mazzara, turned up dead. After that, several of the accused requested to have their bail revoked and spent the remainder of the trial in comparative safety behind bars.

In the end the 'pizza connection' case, as it was dubbed by the press (their twist on the French Connection), closed down one lucrative enterprise, but business went on as usual even while the trial was taking place. Other distribution pipelines were established, the dealers got their cut, the addicts got their fix and the Mafia bosses grew fat and just as smug as before.

Life in the shadow of death

If anyone is still tempted to romanticize the Mafia after reading about organized crime and watching movies about the Mob, they need only listen to Italian journalist Roberto Saviano telling what it is like living under sentence of death for merely writing about the Camorra, the Naples crime families.

For nearly a decade Roberto has been a virtual prisoner, watched by a steel ring of armed bodyguards 24 hours a day, seven days a week, month after month. But the Naples-born journalist is prepared to forgo the pleasures of life that the rest of us take for granted – not the least of which is the liberty to go where we please in peace – in order to expose the cancerous plague that festers under the surface of civilized society from Sicily to New York.

Roberto compares his childhood home in a suburb of Naples to a war zone, where he frequently witnessed innocent bystanders shot dead in the street by Camorra hitmen because they had been mistaken for members of rival families. He is haunted, too, by the sight of grieving widows and grandmothers tearing their clothes in anguish at bereavement. Nor can he forget the acrid stench of urine as a defenceless man wet himself in fear before being murdered in broad daylight in front of witnesses who would never dare to identify the assassins.

At one point there were a couple of murders every day in the suburbs of Naples, as well as firebomb attacks on private houses, shops and business premises. Everyone feared the Camorra, even the police and the judiciary – including those who were not taking bribes. Those who were feared them even more. Saviano, too, was afraid, but he was also angry and his anger overcame his fear. Ignoring all warnings to keep his nose out of their murderous business, he began to ask the questions no one else would dare to ask.

He ingratiated himself with those on the periphery of organized crime in southern Italy: the small fry who ran errands for the underbosses, those who paid 'insurance' to protect their businesses and finally those wary individuals who acted as a lookout when a 'hit' was imminent. Gradually he gained their trust and soon had countless inside stories backed up by trial transcriptions and police reports – enough to fill a book.

Gomorrah

> Since I wrote *Gomorrah*, there's a greater understanding
> of the mafia, and in Italy successive governments have
> been shamed into investing in fighting organised crime.
> They can't pretend they don't know what's going on any
> more, and public opinion won't let them off the hook.
>
> *Roberto Saviano*

In 2006, after years of patient and potentially dangerous investigation, Saviano published *Gomorrah*, an explosive exposé of the sordid and thoroughly unscrupulous and corrupt Neapolitan underworld. It became an instant international bestseller and spawned both a hugely successful TV series and a big screen prequel. At a stroke, it destroyed the myth of the Mafia as smart men in sharp suits who adhered to a code of honour. It also, inevitably, attracted the unwelcome attention of the Neapolitan crime families.

They objected to being portrayed as social parasites: rat-faced, grungy, sociopathic bottom feeders who were exploiting the fatal addictions of the underprivileged and corrupting every stratum of Italian society. But most of all they objected to the glare of publicity their covert activities were now attracting. It was too late to scuttle back under the rock they had crawled out from under. Their only hope was to liquidate the man who had brought their existence to the attention of the outside world.

It began with veiled threats dropped into his mailbox, warnings of what would happen to him if he persisted in his campaign and menacing whispers from strangers who stalked him in public. He then heard that Mafia boss Salvatore Cantiello had threatened his life from his prison cell. Thereafter, Roberto was housed in a windowless room in a police barracks for his own safety. If he went out he was driven everywhere in a bulletproof car, flanked by armed guards.

His life follows a strict schedule which allows for no spontaneous changes to the plan. He has made a few new friends who admire his courage, but he has lost almost all of those he once valued. The simple truth is that no one can afford to get too close to him and he knows it. Travel has become a release, but it is a necessary diversion. He cannot go home to Naples, so his life before *Gomorrah* is now nothing more than a memory.

Roberto Saviano aroused the displeasure of the Naples mafia with his book Gomorrah.

Saviano is not the only Italian journalist living under police protection. There are at least ten more who share his nocturnal world and move nervously from one anonymous hotel room to another, keeping one step ahead of those who have vowed to silence them.

Saviano admits that he doesn't trust anyone any more and that he's afraid of getting close to anyone and letting his guard down, even for a minute. He confesses to feeling constantly under attack, if not physically then as a writer who has sacrificed a normal life to make a stand and whose life has been 'poisoned', as he puts it, to expose the evil that is proliferating unchecked every day.

There is no hesitation in his voice when he says he is not afraid of being killed, only of the pain of a lingering death. Only one thing frightens him more than death and that is that his life will never get back to normal. This is the unknown price that the Camorra and other organized crime families extort from those who oppose them.

I'm constantly accused of trying to make money out of the mafia, of insulting Naples, of making stuff up. It's a way of turning down the volume of what I'm saying. 'We know all this, it's already been written about', that's one of the things they say. If they said, 'None of it's true', we would know they're just mouthpieces for the mafia. But if they say, 'We've heard it all before', it's a more subtle way of undermining me.

It's this fear of being discredited that haunts him when he lies awake in the darkness of the windowless rooms in the police barracks or the cheerless hotel, when he can't tell where he is or what day it is or even the time of the year.

'The fact is, I wrote *Gomorrah*,' he says, 'and I pay the price every day.'

Chapter Seven:
Addicted to Violence

There are rivalries [between drug family cartels] and they seem to pride themselves on being the most feared, the most dangerous, the most violent. And that is dangerous for everyone else.

Former Navy SEAL Adam Newbold

The global trade in illegal narcotics is estimated to be worth more than $300 billion (£236bn) a year. For a slice of that action the South American drug cartels are prepared to kill, torture and terrorize anyone who threatens to get in their way – even members of their own families. In fact, it is frequently members of their own families that they have to crack down on the hardest.

More worrying for those who are responsible for terminating their lethal trade is the fact that the proceeds are pumped into building up ever more powerful criminal organizations and funding ambitious and extensive illegal enterprises. The cartels are also active in kidnapping, extortion and smuggling migrant workers into the United States, some of whom they ransom. And if their families refuse to pay or cannot afford to pay, the abductees are murdered. Los Zetas, one of the largest Mexican drug cartels, massacred 72 migrants when their relatives refused to pay for their safe return, allegedly with the complicit approval of the Mexican police, who were accused of rounding up the migrants and handing them over to the kidnappers. The cartels also siphon money into legitimate corporations, property and natural resources such as gold and crude oil and they fund the market in the sort of high-tech military weapons that would equip a small army.

It's a vicious circle that can be disrupted but never broken.

As soon as the heads of one family have been rounded up and locked away, others emerge to pick up where they left off and they're back in business. It would seem that the government's greatest allies in their much-vaunted but ineffectual 'war on drugs' are the rival cartels, who have been far more successful in neutralizing the opposition. In northern Mexico, the Sinaloa cartel have been particularly effective in reducing the threat posed to their operations by the Tijuana, Juárez and Beltrán Leyva clans, while in the west of the country the Knights

Joaquin Guzman Loera, aka 'El Chapo', is taken away to the maximum security prison at El Altiplano in Mexico City, January 2016. Mexico's most wanted drug lord had been captured by Mexican marines in Sinaloa a few days before.

Templar and La Familia have been seriously weakened by vigilantes and smaller, upcoming rival groups.

When the Mexican military have managed to decapitate major cartels, they simply move into other areas of criminality such as siphoning crude oil from government pipelines and illegal logging and mining. The legalization of marijuana in certain states across the border has not adversely affected their income as they simply diversify into harder drugs with a larger mark-up – heroin, crystal meth and the synthetic opioid fentanyl. The introduction of these more lethal drugs has resulted in a significant increase in US drug-related deaths (up 21 per cent in 2016 to 64,000).

Particularly disturbing is the cartels' discovery of the power of social media. They intimidate informers, activists and journalists by posting graphic videos of their latest executions as a warning to those who might be considering assisting the authorities.

Incredible drug fortunes

> Look at my father's history, all the history he built is in ruins. Nothing is left standing, not him. He lost his freedom many years ago before his death, as did his family as well.
>
> *Juan Pablo Escobar, November 2018*

The violence is inexcusable, but the economics of drug smuggling are understandable. An unemployed and uneducated youth without the money to buy a pair of trainers can turn a $1,500 (£1,180) investment into $10,000 (£7,900) in a single day, provided of course that he can raise the capital. Within a week, if he doesn't get ripped off by his suppliers, or robbed, he can afford to hire a couple of local heavies to help him stake out his own corner and then he begins to make real money. Soon he's carrying suitcases stuffed with cash and is attracting the attention of the men with real muscle and the big cojones.

Not all wannabe drug lords will amass the incredible fortune 'earned' by Colombian cocaine king Pablo Escobar, who was named one of the world's ten wealthiest men by *Forbes* magazine (he was worth an estimated $30 billion/£24bn) and who needed a Learjet just to transport his cash. Nor is anyone ever again likely to attain his 'cult' status, which saw him revered by the Colombians for sponsoring community projects and for his audacious prison escapes, until they learned of the thousands of murders he had sanctioned. Vigilantes put a $220 million (£173m) bounty on his head, which led to a fatal shoot-out with the police in December 1993.

According to Eric Newman, producer of the *Narcos* TV series:

> Years of political corruption and a rich smuggling tradition [found the] perfect product, which was cocaine. It was, pound for pound, maybe the most lucrative substance that's ever existed. It's worth its weight in gold many times over . . . if America was your neighbour and they had an insatiable demand for cocaine, why wouldn't you do everything you could to sell it to them?

Formation of cartels

In the 1960s most of the Mexican dealers were small-time growers who needed white college boy faces to front for them, but they soon resented these marijuana tourists taking a generous cut for 'helping out' their inexperienced brothers south of the border. The Mexicans soon wised up to what they were missing out on and began forming cartels to protect their interests. They weren't going to be screwed by smart all-American crooks, so they recruited from their own families in the belief that they wouldn't have to watch their backs if their brothers, sons, nephews and uncles were there to mind the store while they negotiated deals across the border. The trouble is that the more powerful they became, the more muscle they had to hire to enforce their claim and many of these mercenaries were a little too fond of the merchandise. Whether it's from boredom or the need to stay high in order to kill without conscience, the fact is that many of the killers on the cartels' payroll are permanently high or out of their heads.

The violence has now escalated to the point where the Mexican intelligence agencies are talking in terms of tens of thousands of victims: 83,000 killed between 2007 and 2014.

Role models

In Rio Verde, a small town on the road to Guadalupe y Calvo, they hang human cadavers on washing lines as a warning to those tempted to inform on the cartels. In Guadalupe and the surrounding region, children work in the poppy and marijuana fields with their parents' encouragement, because their sons and daughters are often the only members of the family to be offered paid work. It comes at a cost. Many child labourers die from pesticide poisoning and those who survive graduate to carrying loaded weapons as 'soldiers' of the cartels. The farmers could grow other crops, but the state of the roads makes it practically impossible to transport anything other than drugs if it is to be commercially viable. The huge mark-up on opioids, however, overcomes all obstacles.

It's a disturbing fact that the cartels' operations are not limited to their own turf. Mexican drug cartels are known to have extended their activities to as many as 47 countries, including the United States. As Ioan Grillo points out in his book *Gangster Warlords*: 'Eight of the ten countries with the highest homicide rates are now in the [primary drug] region [Latin America and the Caribbean], as are forty-three of the world's fifty most violent cities.'

And what makes these elusive adversaries more deadly than their predecessors, and seemingly indestructible, is the fact that they appear to have seemingly morphed from the readily identifiable and familiar moustachioed Zapatas of the 1970s and 1980s to what Grillo described as 'a weird hybrid of criminal CEO, rock star and paramilitary general'.

To a generation of youths who only know them from books, movies, songs and violent video games they are larger-than-life self-made Caesars, role models for those impatient young men who would love to be Cuban kingpin Tony Montana in Brian De Palma's iconic 'gangsta' movie *Scarface*. As Grillo observed in a feature for *Time* magazine in January 2016: 'Far more young people idolize Chapo Guzman – the billionaire drug trafficker – than Che Guevara.'

Many of those law-abiding inhabitants who are unable to fight back and want to escape from the war zone try to seek sanctuary in the United States, creating what President Obama called a humanitarian crisis. In 2014, 67,000 of these migrants were parentless children.

That year the Mexican government retaliated in the only way it could imagine might be effective; they recruited former drug lords and any other badasses they could hire to track down and eliminate a formidable cartel known as the Knights Templar, operating in Michoacán. Its leader was a man called Servando Gómez Martínez, whose speciality was a particularly pure strain of crystal meth or

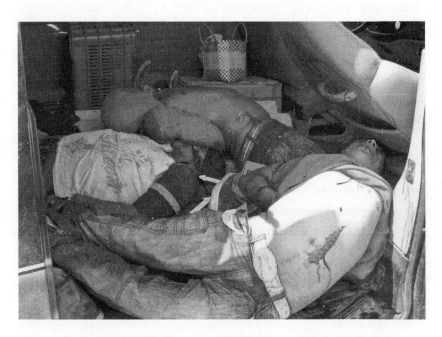

Victims of the Knights Templar gang in La Piedad, Michoacán State, 2013: towns formed vigilante forces to combat the Knights Templar gang and often came off worse.

'ice'. For Gómez Martínez and his competitors hard drugs are not the scourge of the civilized world, turning everyone from students to white-collar professionals into zombies, but a commodity to be marketed and distributed like any other, only not so openly.

But the task force was infiltrated by rival drug traffickers armed with heavy calibre machine guns, grenade launchers and Kalashnikovs, which were not handed out to regular task force volunteers. The volunteers were given AR-15 semi-automatic rifles with restricted firepower whereas the Russian-made AK-47s had been customized to fire circular clips containing 100 bullets. These guys were going to war. And several made no effort to hide their true identity, sporting handguns with their initials set in precious stones.

Los Zetas

One of the most notorious Mexican crime cartels, Los Zetas has even built its own tanks, Mad Max-style, to spearhead convoys of vehicles from which its heavily armed men massacre civilians and ambush regular army soldiers. The Zetas were created from former members of the Mexican Special Forces and army deserters, so they are exceptionally well trained and have a tactical advantage over the regular troops, who are also heavily outgunned. Ironically, the Zetas men were trained in the early 1990s by US 'military advisers' in the expectation that they would be employed to fight the narcotics cartels, not form one of their own.

Los Zetas is active in more than half of Mexico, as it has a grip on 17 of the country's 32 states, while its nearest rival, the Sinaloa cartel, controls 16. Its connection to stateside gangs and organized crime families means that the US federal government is fighting a losing war against an organization that extends far beyond its own killing

Suspected members of Los Zetas from Guatemala and Mexico await the court's judgement on charges of murder, kidnapping and other crimes, Guatemala City, 2012.

ground. Moreover, allegations of corruption have been made against senior political members of the Mexican administration, prompting one observer to remark that it is only a matter of time before the cartel manages to have a member of its own gang appointed state governor.

The Zetas are led by Miguel Morales, a man with a reputation for ruthlessness that is unmatched even in the violent world of the South American cartels. He claims to have personally murdered more than 2,000 people and is known to enjoy watching his victims kill each other with machetes and sledgehammers in gladiatorial fights to the death. But his preferred method of execution is to stuff victims into oil barrels and then set them alight and watch them burn to death.

The Godfather

The alleged participation of Ernesto Fonseca Carrillo, aka 'Don Neto', in the torture and death of an undercover Mexican-American narcotics agent, Enrique 'Kiki' Camarena Salazar, in February 1985 is believed to have been the incident that woke America up to the danger posed by the Latin American drug cartels. It led to the US getting tough with the Mexican administration, which was accused of being both corrupt and apathetic.

'Kiki' was abducted in broad daylight by Mexican police employed by drug lord Miguel Gallardo, or 'El Padrino' (the Godfather). Gallardo was out for blood after one of his largest marijuana plantations, Rancho Bufalo, was torched by the Mexican army on information provided by Kiki, depriving Gallardo of $8 billion a year (worth $19bn/£15bn today). Camarena was tortured for a day and a half before being murdered by having a hole drilled into his skull. He had been kept conscious throughout his ordeal by a cocktail of amphetamines and other drugs, a characteristic method employed by the drug cartels to inflict as much pain as possible on their victims.

Gallardo, a former policeman, was the first of the Mexican drug lords to concentrate on distribution rather than on production and in doing so he internationalized narcotrafficking. Together with his lieutenants Don Neto and Rafael Quintero he established the cocaine routes from South America to the cities of Europe that are still operating today.

He carved up the 'plazas' or territorial units and allocated a specific plaza to each of the major Mexican drug families. The aim was to ensure that each family would keep within its own zone and the authorities would turn a blind eye to their operations, provided the violence did not erupt on to the streets. Gallardo's relatives, the Arellano Félix family, were given Tijuana; the Beltrán Leyva brothers were allocated the Sonoran desert crossings; and the Fuentes family was given the Ciudad Juárez into El Paso.

The murder of 'Kiki' Salazar and the gratuitously sadistic nature of his death aroused widespread out-rage in the USA, putting the White House under pressure to get tough with the corrupt Mexican police and government officials who had been protecting the drug lords, by forcing them to cooperate with the Drug Enforcement Administration (DEA) to bring the perpetrator to justice. America had to be seen to enforce its anti-narcotics rhetoric with action, because such cruelty and contempt for the law could not be allowed to go unpunished. Gallardo was eventually tracked down, convicted and sentenced to 37 years in prison.

Mike Vigil, former chief of international operations for the DEA, said:

> This guy was a ruthless killer. He was an individual that caused untold harm to the United States, to his country, Mexico, and I believe he should be behind bars for the rest of his life. I hope that he stays behind bars, because he truly is a career criminal. He's a psychopath and would continue his destructive ways if he were ever to get out of prison.

Although Gallardo continued to direct his organization from behind prison walls into the 1990s via a mobile phone, his absence created a power vacuum and led to the disintegration of the alliances. In 2006 his protégé, Joaquín Guzmán, declared war on his former associates and claimed the entire Mexican border for himself, including the territory controlled by the Gulf cartel and their feared paramilitary arm, Los Zetas.

In 2016, the 80-year-old Carrillo was transferred from prison where he was serving a 40-year sentence and put under house arrest, due to his age and declining health, but the house he couldn't leave was an exclusive residence in Valle Escondido valued at $500,000 (£395,000).

The Fuentes family

Juárez cartel head Amado Carrillo Fuentes did not die a drug lord's death in a hail of bullets, but of a heart attack on the operating table of a maternity clinic in Mexico City in July 1997, after undergoing eight and a half hours of plastic surgery and abdominal liposuction. The body of the 41-year-old was bloated, disfigured and unrecognizable, so the authorities had to take it away for DNA testing before they could confirm they had finally caught up with one of Mexico's 'most wanted' men.

His death and final journey were humiliating for a man for whom image was everything. He had cultivated the appearance of a successful CEO, owning a fleet of private jets to transport drugs from his headquarters just across the border from El Paso, and is believed to have amassed a personal fortune in excess of $25 billion (around $40bn/£31.5bn today). But he was brought home to Guamuchilito in a tarpaulin because his coffin was too large to fit in the plane.

Although his death was officially attributed to heart failure, there were suggestions that it might have been precipitated by a faulty ventilator or a lethal injection administered by an American DEA agent. There was even a rumour that one of Amado's own bodyguards

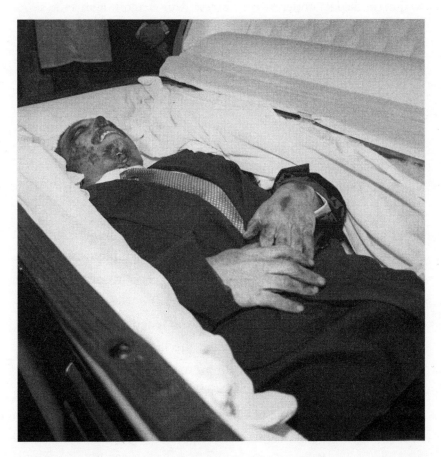

Mexican authorities released this alleged picture of Amado Carrillo Fuentes, perhaps Mexico's most powerful drug lord, in 1997; they claimed he died of a heart attack while undergoing plastic surgery and liposuction to alter his appearance.

who were present in the operating room had suffocated him. Just to be sure, the family eliminated everyone who was present. In November of that year the mutilated bodies of two of the four surgeons were found encased in concrete inside steel drums and bore all the signs of torture.

At his funeral on the Fuentes family ranch journalists were invited and entertained in style, purely because their presence ensured that the family would not be inconvenienced by an army raid. The journalists served as human shields.

'He may have escaped earthly justice, but I'm sure there's a special place in hell for those like him who have destroyed countless human lives,' said DEA chief Thomas Constantine.

Seen as terrorists

Amado was born into a large *campesino* or peasant family, for whom drug smuggling seemed to offer the only opportunity to escape poverty. He was mentored by his uncle Ernesto Fonseca Carrillo ('Don Neto') of the Guadalajara cartel, who sent him to oversee cross-border cocaine shipments and learn the family business from his trusted lieutenants and his *socio*, or partner, Pablo Acosta Villarreal.

The Guadalajara cartel was the seedbed from which many of the next generation of bosses would emerge, those who are now as well known as Hollywood movie stars, sports personalities and other celebrities and whose rise from the backstreets to billionaire status has spawned a glut of books, movies and TV series as well as the *narcocorridos* or 'drug ballads' which 'celebrate' their ruthlessness.

But these men do not fit the traditional image of fictional gangsters. They make no claim to uphold any code of honour and they terrorize their enemies with torture and death by decapitation. The American DEA and the Mexican Security Services consider them to be terrorists, not merely tooled-up criminal gangs, and are determined to eradicate them using the limitless resources now at their disposal.

Bloody inter-cartel feud

Pablo Villarreal was killed in April 1987 in a gun battle with the federal police and the leadership passed to Rafael Guajardo, who was in turn succeeded by Amado.

Soon Amado was overseeing the shipment of five tons of cocaine every month from Colombia with the complicit approval of corrupt officials in the Mexican government, army officers and local and federal police. He could afford to pay them all to look the other way as he was raking in $100 million (perhaps $217m/£171m today) a month smuggling cocaine into the United States.

Amado was as ruthless as they come, but he quickly realized that no man could control such a vast operation without the cooperation of men who would otherwise have been his competitors, men like Joaquín Guzmán, the Beltrán Leyva clan and the Arellano Félix family.

After his death his brother Vicente took over the family business, despite the Mexican government's initial assessment that he 'lacked the leadership and decision-making skills'. That may have been a fair appraisal, but for Vicente it was a matter of family pride. The only men he could afford to get close to him were his blood relatives, his brother Rodolfo and his nephew Vicente Carrillo Leyva.

Under Vicente's administration the Juárez cartel became the most powerful and feared family in Mexico during the 1990s, but the dog-eat-dog competitiveness that characterizes the cartels inevitably led to dissatisfaction within the organization and the trading of insults, which swiftly graduated into the trading of bullets. The murder of Rodolfo in 2004 by the family's former associates, the Sinaloa clan, sparked a bloody and costly feud that continues to this day.

Vicente had a reputation for making unsound alliances and also for striking back hard before he had given himself time to consider the consequences. He is believed to have ordered the killing of Joaquín 'El Chapo' Guzmán's brother, who was in prison at the time of his 'execution'. 'El Chapo', the leader of the rival Sinaloa cartel, predictably took this badly and the feud raged from that day on.

It is a feud which did not end with Vicente's arrest in October 2014. When his brother, Alberto 'Ugly Betty' Fuentes, took over he inherited the responsibility for ending the war, preferably with the extermination of the opposition, but then he too was arrested. And so the shifting alliances and power struggles go on.

To date, Vicente's vendetta has cost the lives of more than 8,000 people.

'Everybody's responsible for this disaster. There are no good guys and bad guys. It's bad guys and really bad guys,' said *Narcos* producer Eric Newman.

The Arellano brothers

One of the most powerful, violent and aggressive drug trafficking organizations in the world.
Report by the US Drug Enforcement Administration

To the affluent, upper-middle-class residents of Puebla, a quiet Spanish colonial city south-east of the Mexican capital, 49-year-old Manuel Trevino was a good neighbour. He had his cars washed every Sunday, he mowed the lawn and he cleaned up after his dogs. As far as they knew his only vice was a taste for expensive cigars, for which he had a particular passion. Those who knew their tobacco could smell the strong, pungent aroma of a Cuban cigar as Manuel stood on the back patio taking his last puff before bed and they must have envied the man who could afford to indulge his habit and do so without having to justify it to his wife. Manuel answered to nobody.

But at 1 a.m. on a Saturday in March 2002 the neighbours were woken by the noise of a convoy of military and police vehicles and a commotion as Manuel was led out in handcuffs to a waiting police car.

Señor Trevino had been living a lie. For nine years he had been posing as a law-abiding citizen while Mexican law enforcement and US intelligence agencies scoured the country for one of the most wanted men in the world. Manuel Trevino was the assumed name of Benjamín Arellano Félix, the man who supplied a third of America's cocaine in partnership with his psychopathic brother Ramón, who had been gunned down the month before. They were known as 'the brains' and 'the brute' of the Tijuana cartel, in which four of the seven Arellano brothers were allegedly actively involved.

Together the Arellanos were charged with ordering up to 1,000 deaths, including those of judges, senior police officers and even a Roman Catholic cardinal, as well as countless witnesses, rivals and innocent bystanders caught in the crossfire of a bloody turf war. It was the assassination of the cardinal in 1993 that forced Benjamín, the head of the family, to go underground. The cardinal had not been the intended target, but the hitmen had botched the job and killed him by mistake. Benjamín might have continued to rake in billions under his assumed name had not the US government passed the so-called 'Kingpin' Act in June 2000, which prohibited American businesses and individuals from dealing with narcotics bosses, terrorists and criminals. It also prohibited US financial institutions from releasing funds and assets held in the name of the designated individual.

Benjamin (left) and Ramón Arellano – two middle-class boys with a penchant for violence.

The Arellanos might have been caught and caged years earlier had not so many government and police officials been on their payroll. It is believed that the brothers paid out a million dollars a week to protect their power base in the Baja peninsula, which was said to be as great as that of the Mexican state.

Traffic

The rise of the Arellano brothers was portrayed in the Academy Award-winning Steven Soderbergh film *Traffic* (2000), one of the first movies to reveal the scale of the illegal narcotics trade across the Mexican–American border. Needless to say, the film toned down the level of violence considerably, but it still managed to shock the viewing public into appreciating the threat posed by the paramilitary cartels just across the border.

At the peak of their power the brothers were smuggling cocaine, amphetamines and marijuana along a 100-mile (161 km) section of the border between Tijuana and Mexicali, using cars and tunnels as well as boats along the Pacific coast.

In February 2002, a month before 'Manuel Trevino' smoked his last cigar in Puebla, US law enforcement officers discovered the entrance to a 1,200 ft (366 m) long tunnel under a farmhouse on the American side of the border, with electric lighting and rails. It had brought billions of dollars' worth of narcotics into the US.

In 1989 the Arellanos had inherited the routes from their uncle, Miguel Ángel Félix Gallardo, the drug lord responsible for the torture and death of DEA agent 'Kiki' Camarena (see box 'The Godfather', on page 259). They had been smuggling TVs, hi-fis and other consumer electronics when Gallardo recruited them and now they had a million dollar narcotics business and no one to answer to. They pressured their producers to increase production and their distributors to sell more product and they multiplied their income until they were raking in billions of dollars a year.

Ramón

No one dared refuse to move the brothers' merchandise and no one defaulted on or delayed payments. Ramón Arellano Félix recruited the bored sons of wealthy Tijuana businessmen who wanted to play at being badass gangsters. They were mesmerized by the sight of him cruising the city in his red Porsche, dressed to kill in a mink jacket and flashing 24-carat gold rings. One of Ramón's acolytes told Mexican narcotics agents: 'In 1989 or 90 we were at a Tijuana corner without anything to do and he told us . . . "Let's go kill someone. Who has a score to settle?"' The informant disappeared shortly after his confession appeared in the Mexican political magazine *Proceso* and was never seen again.

DEA officer Don Thornhill said: 'In my 17 years in this job, I've never seen a more violent group. They would kill people who didn't cooperate. They would kill people who didn't pay a fee or a toll [for moving drugs through their territory]. They would kill people who were not necessarily disloyal to them. They killed them to set an example.'

They even killed their own men, if they thought they might get too big and become competitors. On 17 September 1998 the Arellanos sent gunmen to a fishing village, El Sauzal, to kill their best customer, Fermin Castro, who had always paid what he owed the brothers and on time too. They killed Castro and then almost every inhabitant of the village – men, women and children. Only two survived the massacre.

Ramón was a psychopath and a sadistic one at that. He and his protégés abducted a Mexican prosecutor, his aide and an army officer in April 2000. Every bone in their bodies was broken and their heads were crushed in an industrial press. Two federal police commanders were subsequently charged with complicity in the killings, which they had initially attempted to ascribe to a fatal car crash.

Ramón's death was a fitting end for a man who was out of control and high on violence. He set out to murder a rival, Ismael Garcia, during the Mardi Gras carnival in Mazatlán on 10 February 2002 but was stopped by a police officer for driving the wrong way down a one-way street. When Ramón instinctively pulled his gun, the policeman managed to get off a shot, although he too was hit. That was the official version. The more likely scenario is that Ramón was assassinated by gunmen employed by Joaquín Guzmán, who considered Ramón a loose cannon.

A fortnight later, Ramón's elder brother Benjamín, the head of the cartel, was arrested and the reign of the Arellano brothers was effectively over. In the house in Puebla police found a shrine to Ramón, one of the most prolific killers in Mexican history. Evidently loyalty to Ramón had overcome any reservations Benjamín may have had about his brother being a liability to the family business.

In 2013 the last of the Arellano brothers on the FBI's Most Wanted list, 63-year-old Francisco Rafael, was gunned down by hitmen dressed as clowns at a birthday party in Los Cabos. A spokesman for the DEA had told newsmen that the mood inside the agency was 'ecstatic' on hearing the news of Benjamín's arrest. No comment was made regarding Francisco's murder, but it is doubtful that any of the agents greeted the news with anything other than mute satisfaction.

The Orejuela brothers

The Cauca river, which flows from Popayán in south-western Colombia until it merges with the Magdalena near Magangué, is known locally as the River of Death. So many corpses have been fished out of it that the recovery operation and the cost of the autopsies brought financial ruin to the municipality of Marsella, where most of the bodies ended their journey downstream.

The deceased were almost always impossible to identify as they carried no ID. But from tattoos and other distinguishing marks many were established as being male and female prostitutes, homeless children, street hustlers and petty criminals; the victims of a 'social cleansing' operation sanctioned by the Cali cartel, which was fronted by the Orejuela brothers, Gilberto and Miguel. Hundreds of so-called discardables (*desechables*) were picked up off the streets of Colombia's cities by vigilante groups and summarily executed on the orders of these two men.

However, the brothers were not content with running what has been called 'the most powerful crime syndicate in history' with an annual turnover to rival that of major high street retailers, fast food chains or a major car manufacturing company. They wanted to 'cleanse' Colombia of social outcasts and those whose sexual orientation offended their peculiar religious sensibilities. They had no objection to drug addicts, provided they bought their fix from the cartel which controlled 90 per cent of the world's cocaine in the late 1990s.

What made it possible for men like Gilberto and his younger brother to corner the market in the white powder was a fatal oversight by those who should have known better. The DEA were focused on the heroin trade and dismissed suggestions that they ought to be monitoring the growing use of cocaine by claiming that it was not addictive and had no impact on crime figures or violence.

The Orejuela brothers seized this opportunity to establish distribution cells in the United States which the DEA had little hope of infiltrating or closing down. They were modelled after terrorist cells,

File photo from 1995 which shows cocaine trafficker Miguel Orejuela before he was released by a Colombian judge.

in that none of their members knew of the existence of the other units. Each was answerable to a '*celeno*' (cell boss), who in turn reported to a superior further up the chain. Only this person had access to the cartel, which ensured that the Orejuela brothers could not be compromised by a direct connection to the cells.

Gilberto and Miguel had only one major problem – how to clean their 'dirty' money. They had so much of it that it required a highly sophisticated and convoluted process to launder their billions. The obvious solution was to take control of a bank that could serve as the heart of their financial operations. This they duly did by getting Gilberto installed as chairman of the Panamanian-based Banco de los Trabajadores.

Paper trail

There was no paper trail to help trace the source of the huge cash deposits, nor the interest-free 'loans' and massive withdrawals which funnelled the profits to those who needed to be paid off. And as almost every transaction was recorded and processed digitally, millions of dollars could be transferred around the world in seconds, leaving a trail that would take a firm of specialist accountants years to unravel. The money trail was also obscured by the fact that the brothers had invested in a number of legitimate corporations and set up numerous bogus businesses which they subsequently closed down, to further confuse federal auditors and forensic accountants. These were smart guys and they could afford to employ the very sharpest minds in the financial world, as well as 'black hat' hackers and cybercrime specialists.

As early as 2003 an office of the US Treasury Department, entrusted with monitoring and investigating the foreign assets of those suspected of illegal activities on a global scale, drew up a wall chart illustrating the business structure of the Cali cartel which would have made heads spin in the Microsoft and Apple corporations.

It was not only the cartel's corporate structure that impressed the US authorities but also its highly sophisticated defence system, which had infiltrated the US Embassy and the Ministry of Defence. As early as 1994 the brothers were monitoring all telephone calls out of the Colombian capital. They had men inside the phone companies and were also able to scan their own phones for bugging devices and wiretaps. Even the US government couldn't crack the encryption codes that allowed the cartel to listen in on calls made using the public phone network.

At one point the DEA discovered that their own communications were compromised and their operations within the USA were being monitored by the cartel.

Patient revenge

Gilberto and Miguel Rodríguez Orejuela are as unlike each other as two brothers born from the same mother could possibly be, but they share one characteristic – they are uncommonly, unnaturally patient. When it comes to vengeance, they are in no hurry. No one who betrays the Orejuelas is allowed to live in peace. It's only a matter of time before the brothers exact their revenge and the longer their prey lives in fear of that day, the better they like it.

In late September 1990 almost 20 of the Orejuelas' men, friends and family members, as well as innocent spectators, were massacred at a friendly football game on their ranch in Candelaria. The gunmen had been hired by the leader of the rival Medellin cartel, Pablo Escobar, to put the brothers out of business and he had almost succeeded. A local farmer had aided the killers and it would take the Orejuelas over two years to track him down.

Instead of hiring hitmen, whose presence in the nearby village of Santander would have aroused suspicion, Escobar had paid youths whose arrival went unnoticed. The farmer had provided a base where they assembled before the appointed hour, dressing in army uniforms and tooling themselves up with automatic rifles.

They arrived in two trucks at around 7 p.m., when the game was well under way and the sentries were off guard. Their appearance didn't arouse any suspicions because soldiers often turned up to watch the games, which were played under professional floodlighting and usually featured a professional or two from one of the big regional teams.

In the semi-darkness no one noticed that the military uniforms were an odd assortment of styles and that some of the 'soldiers' were wearing trainers. When they opened fire all the players and spectators could do was scatter. Then the firing suddenly stopped and the gunmen vanished into the night, leaving the dead, the dying and the grief-stricken.

When the police arrived, it was all over. They scoured the area and found two young guys walking along a road, who claimed they had just come to watch the game and were waiting for a bus to take them home to Medellin. But unfortunately for them they were walking in the wrong direction.

Under interrogation the pair confessed and gave up the name of the farm where they had prepared for the raid. The farmer had fled, but his two brothers and his sister were captured, shot in the back of the head and dumped in a ditch. Then the two young men were murdered in their cells by fellow prisoners in the pay of the Orejuelas.

Rough 'justice'

Two and a half years later, the brothers had their man. He had been brought to a ranch owned by one of the four Cali cartel bosses, Hélmer

Herrera, known as 'Pacho'. Hélmer oversaw the money-laundering operation, one of the biggest criminal enterprises of its kind in history, according to the DEA. He was murdered in prison in November 1998.

When Gilberto and Miguel arrived the victim had already been softened up, but not enough to deprive the brothers of the pleasure of seeing him suffer. To their surprise the man did not beg for his life. When they asked him why he had betrayed them, knowing that he would not live to boast of it, he simply said that he had 'made a mistake'. He had no idea what the men who had paid him were going to do and he didn't ask questions. The Orejuelas had one more question, though. Did he know what was going to happen to him now? He didn't reply. What use would it have been to say anything?

It has been said that the brothers left at this point and that 'Pacho' was left alone to mete out 'justice' according to cartel law. But it seems highly unlikely that Miguel and Gilberto would walk away after waiting so long to have their revenge.

The farmer struggled in vain as Pacho's men tied his arms to one vehicle and his legs to another. The vehicles then slowly moved apart, tearing the man's limbs from their sockets. But they still wouldn't cut him loose. The drivers were instructed to reverse and do it all over again. He took 30 minutes to die.

Chapter Eight:
The Children of Cain

It is a common belief that crime and wanton cruelty are inherent human characteristics that have stained human progress since an insanely jealous Cain clubbed his favoured brother Abel to death. But this is not substantiated by history.

It was only after an inexplicable 'leap' in consciousness around half a million years ago – which saw *Homo sapiens* develop a significant increase in the size of the brain and with it an increase in intelligence – that we became self-aware, cunning and ruthless.

Individual acts of killing for personal gain, as opposed to conquest, only appear to have become commonplace once we were capable of rationalizing the act of murder and justifying it to ourselves. Before 2500 BC, killing was largely confined to ritualized sacrifice in order to appease the gods and cannibalism was practised as a means of empowerment.

Certain early civilizations seem to have believed that eating the brains of one's enemy immediately facilitated the assimilation of the defeated adversary's strength and attributes, bestowing power on the victor. It was not an act to satisfy hunger, nor a desire to break a taboo.

In response to unsanctioned killing, the earliest civilizations formulated laws to punish offenders whose crimes threatened the authority of their rulers and their high priests.

A degree of ruthlessness was deemed necessary to enforce the rule of law and the unquestionable authority of the king. Rulers only became tyrants when they ceased to serve their gods and put their own self-interest and sovereignty first.

The first recorded murder trial took place in Sumer in 1850 BC, in order that the accused could have an opportunity to explain their actions and for their fellow citizens to see that those who violated the law would suffer the consequences.

Ever since then we have continued to ask what compels certain individuals to commit premeditated acts of violence and needless cruelty when they know they are extremely unlikely to escape retribution.

Nothing is clearcut. Martin Luther King Jnr, the American civil rights activist, put it this way: 'There is some good in the worst of us and some evil in the best of us.'

Family strife – 'Now Cain said to his brother Abel, "Let's go out to the field."' This image of Cain attacking Abel is on a pillar at Orvieto Cathedral, Umbria, 13–14th century.

The human beast

> Under normal conditions, in their natural habitats, wild animals do not mutilate themselves, masturbate, attack their offspring, develop stomach ulcers, become fetishists, suffer from obesity, form homosexual pair-bonds, or commit murder. Among human city dwellers, needless to say, all of these things occur.
>
> *Desmond Morris,* The Human Zoo, *1969*

In his influential book *The Ghost in the Machine* (1967), Arthur Koestler, the Hungarian-British journalist and philosopher, notes that Man is almost unique in the animal kingdom in lacking 'instinctive safeguards' against the killing of members of his own species. Koestler's contemporaries, Robert Ardrey and Konrad Lorenz, went further by saying that man's innate aggression and propensity for violence was a primary contributor to the growth of civilization. When our capacity for problem-solving has been directed into finding solutions to problems, whether they be related to outwitting an enemy and inventing superior weaponry or more constructive and creative endeavours, civilization has taken a quantum leap forwards, with the result that more progress has been made in the past 100 years than in the previous 5,000.

However, Koestler argued that we are a 'mentally unbalanced species'; an irrational animal whose thinking is fatally influenced by its emotions. We should, therefore, not be shocked by the increasing crime rate that grows in proportion with progress, nor the capacity for 'evil' demonstrated by those who feel excluded from society and are resentful of being made to feel they are insignificant.

Evil families can change if they are determined to do so: Rainer Hoess, grandson of Rudolf Hoess, who was commandant of Auschwitz, campaigns against right-wing extremism. Here he shows a picture of his grandfather and family during the Third Reich.

Caged rats

Earlier studies, such as Quincy Wright's *A Study of War* (1942), have concluded that our ancestors were not naturally belligerent but only became so when herded into overcrowded cities around 5000 BC, where they learned to be distrustful and defensive of their neighbours like rats trapped in a cage.

American ethologist and behavioural researcher John B. Calhoun experimented with laboratory rats in the late 1950s and discovered that overcrowding prevented the dominant rats from establishing and defending their territory, which led to them becoming violent, sexually aggressive and eventually cannibalistic. The dominant rats neglected their natural mating rituals and turned instead to rape and the eating of the young. As with humans, when the dominant minority are denied a means of expressing their dominance in competitive activities, they can become violent and lash out indiscriminately.

More recent studies seem to endorse the widely held opinion among anthropologists that primitive man was not 'a killer ape', but a generally peaceful creature who was unsuited to living in such close proximity to his neighbour and being forced to compete for basic needs.

The more materialistic and competitive we became, the more we craved what our neighbour possessed, with the result that crime has increased accordingly. Most well-balanced and integrated individuals are capable of rationalizing their feelings and make a conscious effort to overcome them by applying themselves to some endeavour that will make it possible to provide for themselves and their families. But others succumb to their basest instincts and indulge their anger, frustration and resentment to the point where they are unable to control it.

Responses to stress

The French philosopher Jean-Paul Sartre (1905–80) propounded the theory that human beings are inclined to see each other as natural enemies and rivals. We resent queuing but grudgingly accept it, provided that the queue isn't too long, and we would prefer to have the countryside to ourselves, but we recognize that this is impossible. Being 'civilized', though, we accept a certain degree of intrusion.

However, overpopulation and severe restrictions on personal space generate stress and the 'fight or flight' response. In extreme cases, where people have low tolerance thresholds this can result in chronic physical disorders or passive-aggressive explosions to release the pressure. When the lemming population exceeds a certain number, the creatures experience a surge of 'fear hormones' which causes them to migrate en masse and can lead to many deaths among the rodents.

Man alone has the ability to control his anxiety, but often chooses not to do so. He will instead find distractions, rationalizations and physical outlets to channel his adrenalin. Those who don't have a suitable and effective outlet either internalize their anger, fear and other 'negative' responses, or they strike out at a convenient target in a desperate effort to free themselves of these self-destructive feelings. Sociopaths, psychopaths and other aberrant personalities lack this degree of self-control and the empathy that prevents more balanced individuals from striking out indiscriminately at others.

As Colin Wilson observes, their 'destabilizing mechanism' has become automatic and a habitual response to stress. The essence of criminality, he argues, is their conscious decision to lose control, to let their heightened emotions determine their actions. They effectively 'boil over' when the pressure gets too much, or they take the easy route, the shortcut to getting what they want without considering the consequences.

Jean-Paul Sartre strolls with his partner Simone de Beauvoir in Stockholm, 1986.

THE CHILDREN OF CAIN

Why people become criminals

> Crime is renewed in every generation because human
> beings *are* children; very few of us achieve anything
> like adulthood.
>
> *Colin Wilson*, A Criminal History of Mankind

Criminality as such is merely 'a childish tendency to take short-cuts', to get something for nothing in the mistaken belief that the perpetrator will always get away with it. As with a child, criminals lack the imagination to see that if they applied the same amount of effort to a legitimate enterprise they would have a greater chance of success and at the same time avoid the risk of losing their liberty or their life.

But a human being cannot be trained in the way that a vicious dog or tiger can be tamed. If violent criminals or sexual predators are harshly punished, they will not automatically resist the temptation to offend in the future, even if they recall that there will be unpleasant consequences. A human being can choose to ignore the chances of being caught if the urge to satisfy their desire is sufficiently strong.

The craving for continual stimulation and excitement is often too strong for such personalities to resist and the act provides them with momentary relief from tension and some degree of satisfaction, comparable in some cases to sexual release. If they harbour resentment for a perceived injustice, or are tormented by the memory of some form of humiliation dating from their childhood, acting out their revenge fantasy on anyone who could be a substitute for their oppressor will offer a degree of grim satisfaction and relief.

And as Wilson points out, 'crime can guarantee success'. A legitimate career requires long-term commitment in order to acquire the necessary qualifications and prove oneself capable and consistent. Criminals do not have sufficient faith in their own ability to earn the trust of an employer, proving themselves worthy of employment and promotion, when it means competing against other candidates and colleagues. As criminals, they do not have to subject themselves to these tests and they do not have to satisfy anyone but themselves.

As Wilson makes clear: 'Creativeness involves a certain mental effort; destructiveness does not.' By committing a crime that makes the headlines, criminals are sticking two fingers up at a society that has refused to acknowledge their uniqueness, or even their existence. Their overinflated egos or sense of self-importance cannot accept rejection and they seek a way to strike back at the world through one individual. The more vulnerable and easy to subdue the better.

Self-destructive impulses

The thief steals rather than working for what he wants and the rapist forces himself on his victim rather than trust in his own ability to seduce her, because he fears that he will be rejected. He needs to exercise power over another person to convince himself that he is not powerless. That is one reason why women, too, can become rapists. Violation and dominance over an unwilling partner are not always committed to gratify the libido.

Once such a person commits a violent crime and gets away with it they soon feel the need to do it again and often the level of violence increases on each occasion, as their jaded senses require greater levels of stimulation. The longer this pattern of behaviour continues the more intense their feelings become, until they risk the disintegration of their personality, at which point they may commit multiple offences in an unconscious effort to be caught and 'rescued' from their self-destructive impulses.

Some of the most successful criminals have uncommonly high IQs, but they continue on their self-destructive path primarily because they lack self-control and have an inflated ego. They have a distorted self-image of themselves as a 'hero' triumphing over their incompetent inferiors, be they rivals or the police, and they are often 'too clever for their own good', as the saying goes, justifying their actions by telling themselves that laws were created to keep the underprivileged and gullible under control. They share a common misconception, namely that Nature is cruel, only the strong survive, compassion is for weaklings and the Universe is indifferent to human suffering.

Childlike mentality

When there are two or more individuals conspiring to pursue a common criminal enterprise there will be a dominant partner and less dominant or subservient associates. The medium dominant partner accepts this perverse philosophy without question, having convinced themselves that the other is their superior in every way.

The admiration of a partner provides the dominant personality with the recognition they require, but it is no substitute for the acknowledgement they seek from society which, paradoxically, they will only obtain if they are caught and their crimes are made public. Charles Manson's 'family' of adoring acolytes and disciples revelled in the publicity and attention the killings had brought them, savouring the outrage their senseless murders had provoked, particularly among the middle-aged 'straights' that they imagined themselves rebelling against.

The painful truth is that certain personality types cannot accept that there is enough for everyone and that they must conform to society's self-imposed rules to earn their entitlement to a share. They simply cannot accept that they will not be 'first', like children who

A photo of Charles Manson from 1970. He once said: 'You have to realize you are the Devil as much as you are God.'

resent their siblings or rivals getting more of whatever is being shared among them, be it sweets, toys or in adult years the material rewards of hard work and the symbols of success. And having a childlike mentality, they want it now.

They are incapable of deferring pleasure as a mature adult would who takes into account that other matters and other people – be it their boss, colleagues or their own family – might have to take priority.

Narcissism

Just as children may misbehave in order to attract a parent's attention, even negative attention can be gratifying to an immature and unstable adult who feels ignored or unappreciated. At the extreme, those individuals who crave attention and have an overwhelming desire to be noticed may choose crime to satisfy those needs, if no other option for recognition appears to be open to them. They either crave to assert their individuality or to bolster their inflated sense of self-importance, what Wilson calls our sense of 'primacy'. It is the self-centred narcissism of the child. Well-balanced adults grow out of it, but habitual criminals are trapped within it.

The violent rages which are characteristic of many gangland bosses exemplify this. They cannot accept any challenge to their authority and lash out like a child having a tantrum. As Freud observed, if an infant had the power to destroy the world, it would. The child and the immature, self-centred adult are both oblivious to the consequences of their outburst, which any normal adult would see as self-defeating.

Most murderers and violent criminals never grow beyond level four in Abraham Maslow's hierarchy of needs as described in his study of human psychology, *Motivation and Personality* (1954). The first is physiological (food), the second is security (a home), the third is belongingness and love and the fourth is esteem. If the individuals who have been the subject of this book had graduated to the next level – self-actualization, the need for self-awareness, the craving to know and understand and create as a means of self-expression – they would have no compulsion to destroy, demean and dehumanize those who threaten their distorted self-image and corrupted view of reality, which invariably leads to self-destruction.

Acting under orders

As Wilson highlighted in *A Criminal History of Mankind*, some of the worst crimes of modern times – the mass suicides committed at the instigation of a cult leader, indiscriminate terrorist bombings and systematic genocide – were not committed by 'evil degenerates' but by those possessing a 'twisted kind of idealism'.

We are not innately cruel, but if we can convince ourselves to see another person as being significantly different – not 'one of us', not belonging to the same race, nationality or type – then we can commit unspeakable acts of cruelty and lack all conscience or guilt for having done so. If we are also empowered by authority to commit acts of cruelty, the majority of human beings would rather commit the cruel act and ignore their own conscience than defy authority. This explains many of the barbaric acts committed by members of a family on their own siblings, when ordered to do so by their domineering parent. All of this was borne out by the famous 'electric shock' experiments conducted by Professor Stanley Milgram at Yale University in the 1960s.

According to an article in *Psychology Today*, Professor Milgram 'demonstrated with jarring clarity that ordinary individuals could be induced to act destructively even in the absence of physical coercion, and humans need not be innately evil or aberrant to act in ways that are reprehensible and inhumane'.

The same pressure to conform to an authority figure within an organization or an institution also applies within the dysfunctional family, where the dominant figure demands blind obedience from the other members. In that potentially destructive and unhealthy situation 'a new creature replaces autonomous man, unhindered by the limitations of individual morality, freed of human inhibition, mindful only of the sanctions of authority'.

The psychopathic personality

> None of the serial killers that I have had the occasion to study or examine has been legally insane, but none has been normal either. They've all been people who've got mental disorders. But despite their mental disorders, which have to do with their sexual interests and their character, they've been people who knew what they were doing, knew what they were doing was wrong, but chose to do it anyway.
>
> *Forensic psychiatrist Dr Park Dietz*

It is a fallacy that all habitual criminals, psychopaths and serial killers are the product of deprivation, abuse and other readily identifiable issues, which contributed to their deeply flawed personalities. The assumption that they could be rehabilitated, or even 'cured', was demonstrated to be patently untrue by two New York psychiatrists, Stanton Samenow and Samuel Yochelson, in 1961. They observed that no matter how much the subject appeared to be willing to listen and to cooperate, they were always able to offer some justification for their crimes; even the vilest child-molester had his 'reasons'. They were also highly adept at withholding anything that might lose them the sympathy or understanding of the psychiatrist.

Samenow and Yochelson were forced to conclude that their subjects were unwilling to change and that they lied habitually both to their doctors and to themselves. They were even unwilling to admit that they had made incriminating admissions in a previous interview, if these contradicted the defence they were offering for their actions in the current session. Their motivation for agreeing to be interviewed by the psychiatrists appears to have been based solely on their need to make an impression and not from any willingness to discover what compelled them to commit violent crimes.

As one clinical psychiatrist once remarked: 'If you try to educate a psychopath all you end up with is an educated psychopath.'

Crime and cruelty

> The criminal is committing indecent assault on society.
> *Colin Wilson*

The distinction between violent crime and needless cruelty, however, needs to be made. Cruelty is often the mindless action of the stupid and unimaginative person who cannot conceive of any other way of forcing another to do their will. As Wilson has observed, it is frequently for the 'savage amusement' of the tyrant or conqueror. Sadism, however, is the wilful infliction of pain for the intense thrill of excitement that it gives to the perpetrator.

'The sadist derives from his act the same feeling of power that the Right Man experiences when he gets his own way by shouting and bullying.'

As Wilson remarked in *A Criminal History of Mankind*: 'It is not a matter of "evil" but of indifference. Most of the mass murderers in history have simply placed their victims in a different category from their own wives and children, just as the average meat eater feels no fellowship for cows and sheep.'

The last word

The violent psychotic at the head of an 'evil' family, like the leader of any malevolent group, is living under a misapprehension. They are deluding themselves that enforcing their authority on others will ensure that they are feared, respected and obeyed. Crime and all forms of aberrant behaviour is ultimately fated to fail because it takes no account of the far stronger impulse to restore order and eradicate or marginalize the offender, the 'rogue' male in the pack.

No better illustration of the ultimate futility of violent repression can be found than that of the Assyrians. In the seventh century BC the Assyrian king, Ashurbanipal, crushed a rebellion led by his own brother, Shamash-Shum-Ukin. The Babylonian ruler committed suicide rather than suffer torture at the hands of Ashurbanipal, who was notorious for the cruelty meted out to his vanquished enemies, but when Ashurbanipal died his enemies rose once again, setting aside their differences to eradicate their Assyrian oppressors. And having learned to be as merciless as their enemy, they slaughtered each and every Assyrian until their fortified and seemingly impregnable cities were nothing more than empty monuments to their former 'glory'.

Within two generations, no one could recall what the Assyrians had achieved. They had conquered all the lands to the south, east, north and west and were masters of the Middle East, but their brutal treatment had not engendered fear, respect and loyalty, only loathing.

As Wilson remarks, they were no longer even a legend. Time and again we see that violence only leads to more violence, until the perpetrator is consumed by it.

FBI profiler Roy Hazelwood has interviewed some of the most notorious serial killers in the course of his career:

> Many, if not most of them, had traumatic childhoods . . . and yes, I have often felt empathy (not sympathy) for the offender. I like to say that my heart bleeds for them as children, however I absolutely hold them responsible for the criminal acts they committed. All of us are given choices as we move through life and our decisions determine the path our life takes. We are all responsible for the decisions we make and this is no less true for the violent criminal. Criminality is not a form of insanity. Criminality is a type of behaviour – illegal behaviour.

The last word on the subject comes from a Hindu sage.

> The greatest error of a man is to think that he is weak by nature; evil by nature . . . What are weak and evil are his habits, his desires and thoughts, but not himself.
>
> *Ramana Maharshi (1879–1950)*

Resources

aboutthemafia.com

americanmafiahistory.com

ancient-origins.net

bbc.co.uk

businessinsider.com

dailymail.co.uk

dailyrecord.co.uk

dailystar.co.uk

drugpolicy.org

gangstersinc.ning.com

glasgowlive.co.uk

gq-magazine.co.uk

heraldscotland.com

historytoday.com

independent.co.uk

insightcrime.org

King Features Syndicate press feature (1935)

listverse.com

livescience.com

macleans.ca/news

mafia.fandom.com

mirror.co.uk

newyorktimes.com

Psychology Today (9 June 2016)

scotsman.com

Sunday People (September 1950)

telegraph.co.uk

thegentlemansjournal.com

theguardian.com

theravenreport.com

therevisionist.org.uk

thescottishsun.co.uk

time.com

unknownmisnadry.blogspot.com

Bibliography

Attwood, Shaun, *The Cali Cartel* (Create Space Independent Publishing, 2017)

Benson, Michael and DiMatteo, Frank, *Carmine the Snake* (Citadel, 2018)

Benson, Michael and DiMatteo, Frank, *Carmine Persico and His Murderous Mafia Family* (Citadel, 2018)

Bingham, Adrian, *Family Newspapers?* (Oxford University Press, 2009)

Burrough, Brian, *Public Enemies* (Penguin, 2008)

Capeci, Jerry and Robbins, Tom, *Mob Boss* (Thomas Dunne, 2013)

Grillo, Ioan, *Gangster Warlords* (Bloomsbury, 2017)

Hernandez, Anabel, *Narcoland* (Verso, 2014)

Kennedy, Helena, *Eve Was Framed* (Vintage, 1993)

Lee, Alexander, *The Ugly Renaissance: Sex Disease and Excess in an Age of Beauty* (Hutchinson, 2003)

Pearson, John, *The Profession of Violence* (William Collins, 2015)

Roland, Paul, *In the Minds of Murderers* (Arcturus, 2007)

Roland, Paul, *Deadly Duos* (Arcturus, 2010)

Wilson, Colin, *A Criminal History of Mankind* (Panther, 1985)

Picture Credits

Index